80 Candles

A Collection of Life Stories

taped, written
and edited
by
Phoebe Smith

far Jan

Phoebe Smith

Published by

**BAINBRIDGE ISLAND
SENIOR COMMUNITY CENTER**
370 Bjune Drive SE, Bainbridge Island, Wash. 98110
(206) 842-1616

Library of Congress Catalog Card Number 88-070827

ISBN 0-9620506-1-X

Book design by Elizabeth Zwick
Cover by John Quanrud

Dedicated to
The Bainbridge Wednesday Writers
for their encouragement
and inspiration

Acknowledgments

The following people have been helpful, and I thank them:

Nancy Rekow who has been my teacher, mentor and consultant and without whom this book would never have been published,

My husband, Chesley Smith, who has given his patience and understanding,

Margi Berger who read and edited the manuscript,

Marilyn Abbott who has helped with editing,

The Operations Committee of BISCC which has been supportive,

Joanne Wills who has provided encouragement and a listening ear,

Elizabeth Zwick who has given generously of her time and skill,

John Quanrud whose art adds so much

The storytellers who were and are a delight, and

Judith Felder who searched and found the

Sponsors

Rotary Club of Bainbridge Island
Group Health Cooperative of Puget Sound
Windermere Real Estate Company/KSH
Felder Construction Company
Puget Sound Mortgage & Escrow
James Decker, C.P.A.
Kitsap County Bank

Table of Contents

Proceeds from the sale of this book will be used to help with the support of Bainbridge Senior Center.

Introduction

80 CANDLES celebrates the lives of ten members of the Bainbridge Island Senior Community Center. All are now or have recently been active in its work. As of 1988, all are in their eighties.

They have lived through the same period of time: horse-and-buggy days, years of do-it-yourself hard work, the Great Depression, two world wars, and the continuing proliferation of machines. Each life, however, is unique. One storyteller claimed she was "just an ordinary person." Although none of the ten has lived an exotic or dramatic life, these stories demonstrate that there is no such thing as an ordinary person.

It was not easy for all of these people to share their experiences because as they grew up, they were often cautioned to keep their intimate thoughts and feelings to themselves. For some, it took courage. Others were encouraged by their children.

Probably not all octogenarians feel like celebrating their lives. Here are ten who can and do.

These oral histories were taped as they were told, then transcribed and edited by

Phoebe Smith

Now that I'm old,
I can be a magician
with white gloved hand
beckoning images from the past.

Once again, I stand on a stage
with my third-grade classmates
all dressed as yellow daffodils
and sing in trembling voice,
"Dear Little Daffy-down-dilly."
I pacify a daughter
on a Grouse Mountain chairlift
surrounded by bees.
I practice my new Spanish
through a white picket fence in Ensenada
with a black-haired boy of seven.

I can wake up in the morning,
roll over and return to sleep.
I can busy myself with memoirs
or sit by the window for hours
watching the clouds play hopscotch
with Mount Rainier.
Saturday comes. Then suddently,
Saturday is here again.

I can say what I think:
scold my grandchildren,
write a letter-to-the-editor
about the ugly house on the corner,
and say no when asked to serve
on the entertainment committee.

I can even paint my toenails green,
or walk backward to church,

now that I'm old.

P.S.

2

Dorothy & Wilbur Nystrom

DOROTHY CAVE NYSTROM is a handsome, well-groomed woman. She is one of those rare islanders who was born in Winslow. It is amazing how many community gatherings she manages to attend, usually with her husband, but not always. It might be a City Council meeting, a B.P.A. performance, Music and Art program or a Historical Society gathering. She is particularly interested in the history of Winslow and has gathered much historical material she may some day put together for viewing.

Dorothy has not taken an active part in BISCC but is one of its strongest verbal supporters.

WILBUR MAGNUS NYSTROM is a tall, slender man whose quiet manner conceals a sharp, inquiring mind. Although he has been a resident of Winslow since 1924 and has contributed to its development in many ways, he is best known currently for his frequent letters-to-the-editor in the *Bainbridge Review* about a wide-ranging variety of subjects that arouse his interest and concern.

One of his charms is a habit of expressing appreciation either verbally or in writing when he thinks it is deserved.

He was secretary on the original board of Bainbridge Island Senior Community Center (BISCC) and later was elected vice-president. He has contributed his tenor voice to the Center's ongoing Gay Nineties Revue.

❧ Wilbur Nystrom ❧

On a perfect garden-party type of Sunday afternoon in August, 1987, Dorothy and I celebrated our sixty years together with relatives and about 280 friends, old and new.

Sunlight flickered through the dozens of 100-foot trees that surround the sturdy, eight-five year old house we have lived in since we were married. We could look down and see the sunlit waters of Eagle Harbor below. A yellow and white canopy, installed in the yard as insurance against rain, added color. A combo of electric guitars, Fretwork, played throughout the afternoon and accompanied Corinne Berg, Anne Fleming and Maxine Wright as they led the guests in singing old-time songs. The Senior Boys' Quartet, so-named many years ago when its members were in high school, sang. Daughter Carol had planned the delicious menu. Grandson, Matt Rothe, videotaped the party, and Theresa Morrow could be seen everywhere snapping pictures. Everyone brought joy and happiness with him or her, it seemed.

We had occasionally joked about this anniversary ever since our fiftieth, but not very often, because we were assuming life was one big adventure and had no thought of aging. However, as the day approached, we began to make mental notes and eventually, preparations.

We needed to clean up our "tobacco road" and gathered together all manner of items to sell, mostly junk with a few antiques thrown in that were probably of more value to us than anyone else. One item was a 1930 McCasty store cash register that a dear

6

old couple packed off between them. Now my wife wishes we had it back. This is the way you become endeared to junk.

The yard needed to be straightened up, the lawn mowed and the garden edges trimmed so it would look like someone lived here. Granddaughter and her husband helped.

It took some doing to prepare a guest list of over 300. We put our old friends at the top of the list, after the family, and finally got the invitations out. They were blue and contained a sketch of our house.

We made a museum of our Blue Room and prepared framed displays of mementos of the past: Grandmother's handwork, World War II, Dorothy's girlhood and my six siblings.

We planned a cruise through the house to see the old Weber piano brought around the Horn from Germany for Dorothy's mother, the carpentry work on the stairway and the eighty-five year old claw-footed bathtub long enough for a six-foot man, and still in use.

There was plenty for everyone to do at the party, and it turned out to be an afternoon to enjoy both at the time and long after.

When the celebration had become a memory, I began to think about how we had made the long trip that brought us to this point.

For me, it all began in Omaha, Nebraska when I was born on December twelfth in 1902, the third of seven children, three boys and four girls. My parents were from Sweden where they had lived on a farm, and were devout Bible students. I grew up with a home life of devotion to principles of doing what is right at all times. When I left home, I found that early family influence was very important. I recommend that all people try to remember that their influence remains in the minds of men long after they themselves move on.

My earliest recollections have to do with running away from chickens in the back yard and learning not to be afraid, with eating dirt when I was hungry and not caring for the taste and with my brother's running away to the shopping center, though my sister tells me I was the culprit who ran away.

Father was the manager of a large grocery store in Omaha. I would sometimes go with him when he travelled in the horse-drawn wagon to visit neighbors and solicit business. He would sit in the kitchen with a housewife and ask her if she needed green onions, carrots or whatever he thought of, and she would tell him what she wanted. He would sit there with a pad on his knee, writing down her order. After these visits, he would go back to the store, fill orders, and in the afternoon, a boy would deliver the grocieries. That's the way we did business. When people came to the store, we had few paper bags, so we rolled paper into cones to hold small quantities. Most products were in barrels—except candy which was in glass jars.

In Omaha, we went to the Swedish Evangelical or Mission Friends Church across town, now called Covenant Church. To activate the pipe organ, the janitor had to pump the bellows. During Christmas programs, I would get to relieve him so he could do other things. Later they put in an electric, eighteen by twenty-inch motor. I got to use my singing voice in church. Before I could read, I could memorize the words of many songs. I wish I could do it now. Once my bossy brother grabbed the book when we were singing a duet, and we dropped it, but we went right on singing anyway. I envied the Reverend Turnquist his rich voice which soared out over those of the congregation. The Sunday school met before church, and Dad was the superintendent.

We moved to another house on a hill. There was a steep drop in the back of the house with a railed stairway going down. I remember wondering what it would feel like to crawl through the railing and fall to the ground. I got my body through, but not my head. If it hadn't been for my sister, I probably would still be hanging there.

We occupied rentals up to this time, and Dad wanted to be more secure, so he bought three lots in north Omaha where he built a house during his off-work hours. I remember his pounding on the other side of the wall when I was trying to sleep. This probably conditioned me to sleeping through thunderstorms or any other kind of noise. Two men came with a twelve-inch screw and drilled a well for drinking water. I guess it was about fifty feet deep; there was good water in Nebraska, and it was cool and delicious. We got it up with a long-handled pump.

We loved to fly kites. We would buy a roll of grocery string we called pea twine for five cents. (Cotton work gloves cost five cents too; real good ones cost ten cents.) Then we'd tie the string to a stake in the ground and watch the kite. Once we saw some boys coming toward us, and we were afraid they would take our kites away from us, so we detached the string and let the kites go and took some joy in their disappointment.

We raised vegetables and chickens. To catch a chicken, we twisted a hook at the end of a wire, sneaked it into the coop and hooked it around the leg of a chicken. There were rats in the back too, six to eight inches long. We trapped them, but also we rigged

9

a barrel of water with a cover that swung out on a swivel. The rat would climb on it, and we would dump him in the water. We were proud of our invention.

I was introduced to education when I entered kindergarten at Webster Public School. There were thirty-five or forty of us, and we sat at desks, two to a desk, The teacher gave us colored paper mats with slits in them. Then we took long slips of different colored paper and wove them into patterns in the mats. I remember how beautiful my finished mat was and how disappointed that the teacher didn't give it proper attention.

In the first grade, I learned there was a process to singing. We sang "do, re" over and over. In fact, after school I would practice it at home until my brother said, "Oh shut up. Youre getting tiresome."

We moved to California Street. The weeds in the back were so high they covered my dad. He got a scythe and cut them down. Then we discovered a mysterious shed. There was a boy at school I really wanted for a friend, so I told him we had a captured animal in our shed. The boy came over, and when he discovered there was no animal, he said, "You lied." That was the first time I had heard the word "lie." My parents had never used the word. I learned the hard way what it meant because that boy didn't want to be my friend after that.

An uncle from St. Paul, Minnesota had seen advertisements about Yakima country in Washington state where they grew apples. Dad was convinced we should go there, so in 1912, we left Omaha and came west. I was a restless eleven-year old and it seemed like an exciting move.

At that time, Yakima country was all sagebrush and smoothed-off mounds typical of eastern Washington. We bought ten acres for about

10

$900, and started planting apple trees. A friend helped us to stake out the land. We planted the trees thirty feet apart, with pear, cherry and apricot trees in between. As the apple trees grew, we then removed the others.

During World War I, we had rationing. For one thing, you couldn't buy a sack of white flour without buying an equivalent sack of a substitute. There was a supply store two miles away, and we would ride over on our cayuse, a strawberry roan, and buy bran flour. We couldn't get Fleischman yeastcake, so we used dry yeast. The bread tasted sour like pumpernickle, and we tired of it, but the neighbors loved it. To bake it, we scrounged the neighboring acres for sagebrush to fuel our Majestic range until we got a team of horses and could go up the mountain and get pine and tamarack logs to cut up for fuel.

We had one cow. It could produce six gallons of milk a day. When it did, we had plenty of butter. But when it was dry, we used prune jam on our pumpernickle-bran bread.

The blacksmith shop was two miles away, so if something broke and needed repairing, we learned to fix it ourselves. Dad taught us all the tricks he had learned on the farm in Sweden. Younger people today, not used to the fix-it-yourself idea, are sometimes impressed by my handiwork. Of course that pleases me.

During World War I, eggs were a premium item. We had gray Plymouth Rock chickens that laid brown eggs. We fed them mashed cull potatoes cooked with midlings or shorts. There were more eggs than we could use, so we took them to the store, and believe it or not, sold them for forty cents a dozen—in 1917!

The first time the whole family had breakfast together, except on Sunday, was when we moved to the farm. In Omaha, Dad had to leave early to get to work. But on the farm, we all had breakfast about 6:00 then worked together from 7:00 to 6:00 p.m. All nine of us sat at a long table to eat our rolled oats. After breakfast, Dad read a chapter from his Bible brought from Sweden. I am most grateful to him for reminding us regularly of the difference between right and wrong because it saved me an awful lot of trouble.

Saturday was baking day. We made enough bread for the coming week. Mother made a huge pancake of bread two inches thick and ten to twelve inches across for Saturday night dinner. It was sliced and served hot. It had a special flavor just like French bread has a flavor of its own. When the eight-hour day became law, it was like a picnic. We could stop work at five o'clock.

During the school year, we went down in the valley to Marks School, named after the man who had donated the building. There were nine grades. My eighth grade teacher, Nellie Short—still alive the last I heard—had suggested that a girlfriend and I skip a half grade. When graduation time came around, I learned I was to be tested on square root, and I had missed that. So Miss Short taught me square root the night before the exam. I missed a lot by skipping. It has vexed me ever since. In the ninth grade, I had trouble with algebra although I liked geometry. In the same grade, I asked Mr. Barton a question, and he said, "Let's go look it up." We did, and I had a lesson in self-reliance. Outside, we played soccer, baseball and tennis. There was a privy in back. Winters were wet and muddy. Summers were dry and dusty.

When I was in the ninth grade, Dad suggested I stay home and help him on the farm. In those days, a suggestion from your parents was an order. I dropped out of school for two years and worked with Dad.

While the orchard grew, we planted cash crops between the trees. We raised carrots, corn and potatoes. In the fall, a potato digger pulled by horses dug the potatoes which we put in oil cans or buckets, then dumped them unwashed into bags. We got $20 a ton for them. There were twenty sacks in a ton, $1 a sack, a penny a pound. When times were better, we got $40 a ton, and thought we had hit the jackpot. We hauled them in wagons to the interurban terminal in Wiley City two miles away, named for the Wiley family which owned extensive farms nearby. We delivered the potatoes to the boxcars and got credit slips we cashed in later.

Some of the carrots and corn we fed to the chickens and pigs. We had two kinds of pigs, Berkshire and Poland China. The latter grew large and were mostly fat four inches thick. I liked fat pork. In winter we froze it and sliced off pieces to eat. For me, a delight even today is cold pork with mustard on it.

When I was twelve or thirteen, my brother and I and a friend walked down to Ahtanum Valley, up the other side, and down to the next valley where there was a sheep-borning camp. When we got there, we asked, "Do you have any bum lambs today?" A bum lamb was one of triplets. A ewe would only care for two, so the third was expendable. We took two, a Lincoln with long wool and a Berkshire with black ears and much shorter wool. In return, we gave the sheep man an apple. He seemed pleased. We walked up and down hill for the five miles to home, carrying those lambs and didn't even know we were tired.

Our friend took one of the lambs. We raised ours with the cows. When the lamb was old enough, we took it to Wiley's to have it bred. Both the ewe and the buck disappeared. We climbed on our cayuse, Dick, and looked all over for them and finally found them in the barn of a neighbor who was planning to keep them. The sheriff gave us a search warrant, and the man gave up the sheep. He was cited before the justice of the peace and fined ten dollars. Justice was quick in those days. We figured that since the lamb had been raised with cows, she didn't know what sheep were and was frightened by the buck and ran away. And the buck ran after her.

The ewe had twins, and we were in business. The twins matured and mated, but they weren't afraid because they knew what a sheep was. When the war ended, the price of wool was good, but we sold our entire flock to Wiley anyway. A week later, the price dropped, and we congratulated ourselves on our keen business sense.

We had a team of horses. One of them was named Humpy because he had a small lump on his back. The other was Babe. Humpy caught his foot on a barbed wire fence and almost cut it off. I wouldn't let Dad shoot him because I hoped I could cure him. I gave him a soda poultice every day until the foot healed. I had a good feeling about that. That team of horses was still there when I left the farm.

After working on the farm for several years, I was persuaded by a friend to go to high school in Yakima twelve miles away. I was seventeen. At the high school, they searched my records and found what I needed to complete the course. I majored in commercial subjects and was strong in English and history. I liked debate and music, but because I lived in the country, I never got into sports or other extras. The school didn't recognize my music talent so never pushed it to its finest conclusion.

Because I was older than my classmates, I was able to absorb learning better and appeared to be smarter, a fact my younger siblings found hard to accept. It took me two and a half years to complete the four year course, and when I did, I became a charter member of the Yakima High School honor roll.

At first I walked two and a half miles to the interurban and took a bus to school. Then I got a job as a bus boy with a travelling salesman and his wife, Whit and Mabel Routh. We became friends. Mabel had a girlfriend named Dorothy Cave who lived on Bainbridge Island and was going to college in Bellingham. Mabel thought Dorothy and I might enjoy each other, so I wrote her a humorous note that was the beginning of a long correspondence.

To furnish a cash flow, I did odd jobs that included cleaning a flower shop every day for which I received ten dollars a month.

The summer I finished high school, my younger brother, Paul, had a 1916 Chevrolet that ran. It had no top, but it ran. We decided to drive to Puget Sound to seek our fortunes. We got as far as Issaquah when the back axle broke. We bought an axle for eight dollars, and right then and there, repaired the car ourselves.

Then on to Seattle. When we arrived, the sun was setting. That night it rained, and the next day, the sun shone again. We thought we had reached heaven. We stayed with a friend who had some acreage north of Seattle. There were lots of downed cedar trees, so for a while, we rustled shingle bolts from the woods.

Then I saw an ad in the paper for a secretary to a logging company near Olympia. I applied successfully. The company shipped trainloads of logs, and my job was to keep track of them, to do the books. Later, I also audited the books of the company store.

While working there, I met Dorothy. I made an appointment to go to Bainbridge Island and caught the steamer, *Bainbridge*, at Pier 3 in Seattle. The boat was captained by Cyp Wyatt, and Oscar Lundgren was the mate. We landed at the Winslow dock where the Saltwater Cafe is now. As the steamer pulled in, I saw Dorothy on the dock. We had been corresponding for so long we felt we knew each other well. She and her mother invited me to the house, the first of many visits. Her mother and I got along famously. We were both bookworms and enjoyed discussing fictional characters. She was a marvelous cook and could make boiled potatoes taste really good. Or did the atmosphere surrounding the visit have something to do with it?

The Olympia job became boring, so I decided to go back to Seattle so I could go to night school. I worked days as manager of a company making laundry machines and went to school at night to learn accounting, law, economics and marketing. The job ended, so I found one as a statistical clerk and desk salesman at the Goodyear Rubber Company. I stayed there until 1929 when the Depression hit, commuting from Bainbridge after our marriage in 1927.

We had been engaged since 1924, and our wedding took place in Dorothy's home. Her father, having been a florist before the turn of the century, decorated the living room magnificently. Robert Cave was one in a million, intelligent, active and alert. He was one of the key community-minded men and popular. He hated to see his little girl get married. It was a real challenge to him, but he rose to the inevitable and was a truly good sport. He delighted in throwing rice on our Model T Ford coupe when we drove away, and in the wet weather later in the year, we had rice trim in the joints of the automobile body.

In 1930, Clinton, my brother-in-law, wanted to go into the retail business on the island, and he needed a partner. The general store was a success, and eventually we expanded into five stores at Winslow, Port Blakely, Manitou Beach, Port Madison and Creosote—the Cave and Nystrom stores. In 1936, we separated. I took the Port Blakely store and Clinton the others. In 1940, I sold out, and after a short stint in Bremerton, we moved to Seattle.

I wanted to take part in the World War II effort but was over age so became a 4F. For a while, Alaska was closed and families evacuated for fear of a Japanese invasion. After the danger subsided, I went to Kodiak on the old freighter, Denali, and I was storekeeper for the United States Navy, starting out in a big quonset hut. Everything was new. No one knew how much of what was going to be needed, so one gross of everything in the book was ordered. We had some items that were so plentiful they could last for several wars. Others had to be reordered and shipped in by plane in a hurry.

Navy officers were put in charge and got many ratings because of their education, not their experience. These so-called merchandising experts we called "feather merchants." Our enthusiasm turned to frustration because of military inefficiency, but we did the best we could.

It was a joy after the war to get back to the wholesale business selling carloads of produce like potatoes from Minnesota and North Dakota. It seemed like such worthwhile and necessary work. Then came the squeeze of competition, and I was out of work again.

In 1946, we moved back to Bainbridge, and from there I commuted to a new position with Wendell West Real Estate Company which had forty offices all over the United States. I supplied them with office and promotional materials until 1972 when I retired to enjoy our Winslow Shangri-la.

In addition to my work, I got involved in community affairs. I could write a book about the growth of Winslow from 1924 until now; from several hundred people to thousands, from dirt and gravel streets to paved roads, from houses with individual wells and septic tanks to complicated water and sewer systems. There was the fight over the Agate Passage bridge. There was the evacuation of the Japanese during the war. Maybe someone will write this story some day. But let me tell about what I did to make it all happen.

In 1947, Winslow incorporated. George Thompson, a Standard Oil man, was elected mayor. He called me and said, "We need a planning commission. Would you serve?" I did, as secretary, for sixteen years. The committee had seven members, and Bert Stretch was the chairman. We were just ordinary people and needed to learn about zoning, building, laws, etc. So we went to Bellevue to get a copy of their comprehensive plan to serve as a guide for ours. We started in planning a city. I remember we thought we had done an excellent job when we worked out the zoning. Lots in the Hawley district were small, so we zoned them 7,500 square feet and then 12,500. Of course, it's all changed since then.

The justice of the peace resigned. I was asked to take the job. "Why me? Why not a lawyer?" "Because lawyers don't want to do it." Well we had to have such an officer to handle traffic problems, some disturbances and occasional suits. So I went to Fred Grow and asked him how to proceed. "Just like I do my job. Find out for yourself," he said. I wrote to the county auditor and received some blank journals. So all I had to go on was common sense. When the county clerk, a religious man, complained about the question, "Do you swear?" I changed it to "Do you affirm?" One business man who hadn't actually visited the court, thought I wasn't firm enough and referred to the "Mickey Mouse Nystrom court." Another didn't want to be in my court because he "didn't want another lecture." This because I tried to reason with people to make them more careful.

I became the police judge also—justice of the peace for the county, police judge for the city, both in the same office. Clients paid two dollar fees. I made from twenty to fifty dollars a month, though some of the penalty fees had to go back to the county. Then a new state law was passed requiring that this work be done by lawyers, so I was released from jobs I had done for twelve years.

In the 50s, we had a new but active Chamber of Commerce. Jack Gordon was president, and again, I was secretary. We met at night in the office of the *Bainbridge Review* which had its plant in the shipyard. Eventually, we had enough business to install a telephone. It still has the same number, 842-3700. I have a program of a dinner put on by the Chamber, titled "Goodwill Roundup," which was attended by two hundred people. On the program, I can read, "Remarks: 'The Chamber as a Bainbridge Island Catalyst' ...Wilbur Nystrom, Secretary, B.I. Chamber of Commerce."

After retirement, I still kept busy. I was appointed to serve Kitsap County as chairman of the Board of Equalization, a five-man group that evaluated situations where property values were perceived as being questionable. One interesting case was the Indian effort to reclaim tidelands on the reservation.

For many years, I have enjoyed being affiliated with the Christian Science Church. I strongly share its beliefs. One is that though we often think of life in terms of time, what is really important is the way we spend that time.

Another observation resulted from a trip we took to the Holy Lands and Egypt five or six years ago. We went to reinforce our understanding of Bible history, and we did. But we also saw how people lived and came to the conclusion that people are pretty much the same all over the world.

I plan to spend my eighty-fifth birthday in Hong Kong examining its history, art and culture first hand, with a group of other Americans. Who knows? Maybe I'll come to some more conclusions.

Most of what I've said so far could be called history—his story. The big part of my whole life is her story which she can tell for herself.

❧ Dorothy Nystrom ❧

"Next to being a jazz saxaphonist, I wanted to be a nurse."

It was a windy, stormy day on March 29, 1904 when Dr. Kellam, the only doctor on Bainbridge Island at the time, drove over to our house from Port Blakely in his horse-drawn buggy to deliver me. I was born into a nice warm home where I was loved and enjoyed, even by Clinton, my older brother, who always took an interest in taking care of and playing with me. I felt protected by him and my parents. Maybe that's why I grew up feeling free and happy. I was probably spoiled. I certainly don't remember any feeling of pressure. I felt like I could do anything I wanted to. I didn't seem to want to do anything malicious or mean. Could that be why my parents handled me with such a loose rein? I seldom did work around the house like dishes and cleaning. I didn't know anything about that. Mother did it all. Clinton and I never did a thing but play—after school, of course.

Before I tell you about me, let me introduce my parents. My Father, Robert Cave, was a stocky medium-brown-haired man with blue eyes and a British accent learned in Boston, England where he was born. I remember him as fastidious because every day he went to the barber shop in Winslow for a five cent shave. Mr. Masaaki, Johnny Nakata's father, was the barber.

When he was fourteen, Dad had decided to come to America. This distressed his father, a horticulturist who grew grapes and flowers for the King and Queen. When Dad left home, the family gathered and sang songs. Dad brought a love of music and beautiful tenor voice to this country.

He landed in New York and worked for Peter Vaughn who ran a famous seed place. Dad worked until he had saved enough money to build his own greenhouses. To do this, he moved to Akron, Ohio to join a young friend from England, and together they built and operated their greenhouses for several years until the greenhouses burned down. They never knew exactly how it happened.

Then he heard Seattle was a booming town, so he went there and met Edmond Meany, later to become Professor Meany at the University of Washinton. The two of them built greenhouses where the Civic Auditorium now stands. In 1889, the Seattle fire destroyed those greenhouses too. Dad then started one of the first Seattle florist shops, on First and Marion. He also helped to organize the state's first florists' association.

In the meantime, he had bought property on Bainbridge Island where Ferncliff and Winslow Way meet because he wanted his father to come over from England to live with him. His father did come, but he only stayed a week. At the time, the trees had been cut to supply the mill, and the property was all stumps. Dad's father was used to the beauty of the Lincolnshire countryside in England, and he couldn't stand the "ugliness of Bainbridge Island."

When he was married in 1898, Father built a big house for his bride, and it was called the Honeymoon House ever after. It had a big upstairs, three bedrooms downstairs, dining room and library from which stairs led to the upper floor. There was no laundry, so later one was built, as well as a bathroom. The house had running water that was stored in a tall tower. The house still stands and is rented to a dance studio. Some day I want to restore it and make it a Winslow masterpiece.

Father built his greenhouses from which he shipped tons of produce all over Alaska. He also managed the Port Blakely Mill gardens which supplied produce for the workers and ships. To get to work, he walked around the head of the bay through Eagledale until he got to the gardens.

Because of his occupation, we always had the very best of everything to eat at home—meats, homemade white or oatmeal bread, and certainly fruits and vegetables.

Dad was always interested in politics. He was a died-in-the-wool Republican and on a first-name basis with many other Republicans in the state. I was aware very early of political discussions at home and of Dad's activities in politics.

Mother was a dignified lady whom people mistook for English though she wasn't. Her accent identified her with San Francisco where she lived. She came to the island in the first place to visit her brothers who ran the Hall Brothers Shipyard. Father always had her support in politics though she herself didn't belong to organizations, except for the D.A.R. With friends, she was friendly but choosy. She was an intelligent conversationalist—didn't yak around like I do.

Music was always an important part of our home life although Clinton and I didn't get a bit of it. Wilbur says my music is in my feet because I always loved to dance and still do. I did study piano until I was a senior in high school. I still have the announcement of my final recital.

Holidays were important to our family too. July 4th was celebrated much as it is now only on a smaller scale, and of course, there was much more room to celebrate in. People came over from Seattle for the fourth and also to dance at Fosters' in Fletcher Bay. It was the hottest spot on the island at that time. Mr. and Mrs. Foster were great people and conducted a very strict dance floor inside. Outside, however, there were cabins to rent, a store on the dock and many places to make mischief.

Each Christmas, Dad went beforehand to the commission house where he sold his produce and brought home a crate of oranges, a stalk of bananas, and boxes of figs and dates. Clinton and I would get up at 4:00 a.m. to see what Santa had brought us. I usually got a new doll with its own equipment, books and clothes. Once I found a lovely doll buggy under the tree. My brother's favorite gifts were his bicycle, baseball bat and gloves. Later, friends would come over to see our gifts, and then we would visit them to see theirs. Dinner, though, was a private affair, though sometimes we invited Mr. Hall, who was the son of the shipyard owner. I remember him as a fine, well educated gentleman. The table was beautifully set—very proper.

One of my earliest memories sees me riding around in my baby buggy, pushed by my brother. I kept that buggy until about five years ago, when I loaned it to someone, but can't remember who it was.

As I grew older, I wanted a baby sister or brother because my chum, Dolly Wyatt, had a baby sister, Snookie. Since I didn't have one, I adopted the neighbor babies of Laurella Routh and of Frank Shepard. Every day after school, I went to Routh's house or Shepard's to play with the babies. I wheeled them downtown in their buggies. I was a big shot then. I guess I was ten or eleven. I always have loved children. That's one reason I eventually made a good teacher. I was really fond of my pupils.

They became my kids.

Later in the seventh and eighth grades, along with my girlfriends, I became boy-struck. We each had a boyfriend. Every month we had a dance in a private home—either the Wyatt house, the Meyers house, the Metcalf, the Rogers or the Island houses. We didn't take dancing lessons. We just learned from each other. We danced. That's all—just danced. Kids today just don't know what fun is.

From going to community dances where there was an orchestra, I got acquainted with jazz and the saxaphone. I wanted to learn to play a sax, but it was one thing I was not permitted to do. It wasn't ladylike. Besides, at that time, jazz was looked down upon, and my classical piano teacher said no to the very idea.

I loved tennis and got very good at it. I played baseball—all sports. We weren't forced to do anything, just took our choice. Every day was a day for fun.

I enjoyed high school but not the subjects. I wasn't a student. I was a disrupter and liked to cut up. Victoria Yankowski of a Russian family in Eagledale was my chum. What she couldn't think up, I did. Anything to upset the calm of school was the order of the day, like going to school with your clothes inside out. I giggled so much in study hall, the teacher often had me go up to the front of the room and get under her desk. When I was sent to the principal's office, he said."Dorothy, you're here too often. Go back to class and behave." I guess he ran out of ideas of what to do with me. Every once in a while, even now, I meet a former classmate who says, "Dorothy, do you remember when....?"

I couldn't get geometry through my head, so when I had to prove a theorum on the board, Victoria dictated from the front seat what I should do and say, a step at a time. We really worked together even when we were cheating.

Jim Murray was a strong leader, and he and Victoria and I set the rules. We had one teacher who was old, maybe thirty-five, and wore a wig. Her name was Miss Hogg. We decided because she was old, she deserved respect. so we set out to learn English. It was the only class we took seriously.

When we were graduated from high school in the community hall on Cave Street, named after my father, we girls wore new white dresses and carried bouquets, and the boys wore suits. Everyone dressed up in those days for special occasions, not like today. There was a program, the usual valedictorian and guest speakers. I didn't get any scholastic honors, but I did play the piano, I remember.

After high school, my brother insisted I go the the University of Washington to get acquainted with college life. I started to study interior decorating but decided it would take too long to become independent and make my own living. Next to being a jazz saxaphonist, I most wanted to be a nurse. Mother couldn't stand the idea of my being exposed to blood and all that disagreeable stuff. She wanted me to teach piano, but I was off music because I couldn't study jazz. There were only three things a woman could do in those days other than marry and raise a family—nursing, teaching and being a secretary. It was beneath me to be a secretary, so all I could do was teach which didn't seem like too bad an idea since I did like children. Besides, it was only a two-year course at that time. So Victoria, who went to Ellensburg, Myrtle Sarin and I, who went to Bellingham, became teachers.

After college, we all looked for jobs. Through a

Bellingham friend whose mother was head of a Seattle Pacific College dormitory, I heard of Mr. Damon, principal of a school at Quincy, Washington over near Moses Lake. He needed a combination first and second grade teacher. I got the job, and when fall came, got on the train for the all-day trip to my first teaching position.

I didn't know very well how to teach, so when at the end of the first month, Mr. Damon brought me report cards to fill out, I said, "I haven't been doing all these things on the card, and what I have been doing I haven't really kept track of. I can't possibly make out these cards." "Would you like me to come down and help you?" asked Mr. Damon. He came to my room every day for a month and taught me how to teach. At the end of the month, he said, "You're on your way, and you're going to be a good teacher, Dorothy." —and I was.

I sometimes accompanied the high school basketball team to neighboring towns like Hartline and Ephrata. Mr. Damon was strict on the behavior of teachers. He told us how we should take the team to town, what time we should get back and how we should act. We kept the team in order. There was no monkey business.

After school and after supper, some of us played tennis. There was the barber, another teacher named Smith, John Greenley and I. We put on a good show for the people who often gathered to watch. We should have charged admission, but we didn't. This even went on in the winter and all day Sunday. It was our exercise and our entertainment.

I taught in Quincy for three years. Then I taught in the Bremerton area for two more years. I lived at home on the island and took the ferry from Point White to Bremerton and then another ferry to

Manette. In winter, I sometimes stayed near school over the weekend. The ferries were filled with working men going to and from work. I played cards with them. I guess I played my way through life.

I had been corresponding with Wilbur for some time. Occasionally he came over to Quincy to see me, and I saw him when I came home. While I was in Bremerton, he was working in Seattle, so he came over to the island weekends. We were engaged in 1924, but it wasn't until 1927 that we were married.

The wedding was at home and enjoyed by 100 friends and relatives. Dad decorated the house with flowers. The minister, Dr. Graham, from Quincy came over to marry us. Mother had engineered supper on the porch after the ceremony. I wore a borrowed handkerchief, a blue garter, a long veil and my grandmother's brocaded silk wedding dress with a pearl yoke.

After the honeymoon in Vancouver, B.C., we returned to the island, and Wilbur started to commute to Seattle to work. I continued to play tennis, visit Mother down at Honeymoon House, and she came up to visit me. Learning to cook and plan meals was absorbing. At first, I didn't know about proportions, and the first time I baked beans, I used a whole can of molasses. Wilbur still teases me about that. Evenings, Wilbur and I often played bridge with other couples. In fact, we had a club. Each time, the hostess would try to outdo the last one until bridge parties became banquets.

When Carol was born, I insisted on staying home for the birth because I was afraid I might come home from the hospital with someone else's baby. I told Wilbur, "If the baby's a boy, he will be a husky football player. If it's a girl, she will be beautifully dressed, a showpiece." I raised her pretty much as I was raised. She was not a child who pulled at tablecloths. She learned to look at things but not touch, and that everything has a special place. We had formal dinner parties, and Carol was always included. I gave her as many forks and spoons as anyone else. I taught her in advance of the party how to use them. In those days, children were "seen and not heard." She learned that. Later, when she went away to college, she wrote and thanked me for the social skills she had learned at home because some of her friends hadn't been as lucky.

We sent her to Whitman College because a friend of mine had gone there and thought it would be just right for Carol. After her third year, she came home and announced, "I know what I'm going to do—teach." I had no idea that's what she was planning, so I said, "Oh, no! Well, if that's what you want, you're not going to graduate from Whitman." I learned that Ellensburg in central Washington was the best place to learn to teach, so we sent her there, and she graduated. For a time, she taught at Highline, north of Seattle, and then at Selah near Yakima. She has been in education ever since while, with her husband Donn Rothe, raising Sarah and Matt.

Interest in community affairs was an extension of my childhood. I once told someone, "I was born a Republican." Wilbur had his own ways of being involved in the development of the island and of Winslow. My special interest has been the Historical Society and preservation of some of the fine accomplishments of the past. I am a member of the D.A.R, the Garden Club, and on the lighter side, I support Music and Arts and the Bainbridge Performing Arts, formerly Bainbridge Light Opera— although not as a performer.

In the early days, there was no city council or even a chamber of commerce. If we wanted improvement, we had to get it ourselves. A group of people who knew how to work together would come up with an idea and carry it through, each person contributing his or her own particular skill. This is the way we got a telephone system, electricity, the Agate Passage bridge and a public hall.

Boys were playing basketball in a barn, and they were winning games with neighboring towns. We decided they deserved to have a better place to practice. So we built a public hall at the end of Cave Street. It's not there any more. Each one of us gave what we could to the project, whether it was carpentry, fund-raising, lumber and other supplies, painting—whatever. We all pitched in and built a hall that was useful not only for young basketball players, but also for political rallies, dances, graduations, plays and occasionally a Seattle choral group of fifty, the Anthem Society. It was a real community center, and we were proud of it and of each other. Nowadays, we pay to have needed facilities built. But in those days, when we wanted something, we took care of it ourselves. It was fun, and it made for a strong feeling of togetherness and cooperation.

When Carol was in her teens, I returned to teaching, first in Seattle and then back on Bainbridge where I first had a grade one at the old Mac-Donald School in Eagledale. Then I worked at the Bainbridge Elementary School, now Commodore Bainbridge Middle School. For five years, I taught remedial reading in all of the schools.

After I worked with remedial reading for a year, I thought it would be better for the program in the long run if I could start at a lower grade, the third. This was a period when sight reading was in vogue, and I felt it was important to stress phonics. The principal gave me permission to do this when I explained that if we did, we could probably eliminate remedial reading in five years. I had to organize the work and classes carefully because I had 149 students whom I taught four days a week. The vocabulary I used came from the readers the students would use in their regular classes, and I taught the words phonetically. At the end of five years, I only had five boys left with reading problems. I wanted to put the boys to work on a janitorial project I thought would motivate them to learn better. The principal had a different idea that I couldn't go along with, so I returned to teaching first grade. I am proud of some of the students who began to develop their talents in my first grade, including Ralph Munro, Washington's Secretary of State. After twenty-four years, I had to retire because I was sixty-five years of age.

After retirement, I organized the first preschool education program on Bainbridge and it proved to be very successful.

The Women's Civic Club made me its president. Winslow Way is more attractive because of its efforts. Wooden benches in front of the American Marine Bank and other spots and the brickwork on which they stand, the nine trees along Winslow Way, a garden that leads to the post office, blue awnings and the scene painted on the Beach Building at Winslow Way and Highway 305 are all inspirations of the Civic Club which disbanded about a year ago.

In the shadow box museum at the Winslow Mall are photographs of some of the men who started the town of Winslow. Their sons are among those who formed a group they named Pioneer Alumni Association. I presided over the group when it established a monument on the corner of Winslow Green in memory of the first combination grade and high school on the island, that was located on that site.

In 1979, we flew to England to find out more about my family background. For some reason, I had thought my family members were poor, but I found they were all successful teachers, artisans and jewelry makers. After the long flight from Seattle, we were met at Heathrow Airport by a cousin who worked at the airport using her knowledge of several languages. She helped us get our bearings in and near London. Then we went to Edinburgh, Scotland and located Cave Castle which I had heard about. For many years it had belonged to my ancestors. Then one of them joined Brigham Young in America and disappeared. When this happens in England, the property reverts to the Crown. From there we went to Boston, the original one in England, and visited the church my father had attended, the Boston Stump Church. We climbed to an old steeple, still after hundreds of years, lighted for sailors at sea. Docks at the small Boston harbor were packed with boats from Italy, Russia and France—all loading produce.

We decided to go to Plymouth, England to trace the Pilgrims who came to America. "You don't want to go to Plymouth. You want to go to Billericay. That's where the Pilgrims were," we were told. So we went to Billericay about thirty miles north of London and discovered how the Pilgrims had lived, what they ate, how they got away. We saw the tunnel they had built under the street for escape if necessary. When we got home, we looked at a family record book Mother had kept and found our family had started in Billericay. Later, in Boston, Massachusetts, we learned my ancestors had come to America on the Mayflower.

Our home is the focus of our lives. It was built in 1902 by Jacob Miller for his wife. We bought it to move into when we were married in 1927. The house is filled with items we have collected through the years that remind us of the past of Winslow, our families and ourselves. It is our own private little museum. We love every bit of it, the marine paintings on the stairway walls, bound magazines from the 1880's, Mother's Weber piano shipped around the Horn for her, the old-fashioned heavy oak furniture, and much more.

Recently we built on the back of our house an addition of several rooms that are modern and convenient, but we still live all over the house. The builder, on examining the stone foundation, discovered the house hadn't moved one half an inch in eight-five years. It was so carefully constructed of one inch vertical grained lumber from the Port Blakely Mill that the joints look as if they were one piece.

When we moved into the house, the trees were about twenty-five feet tall, and we could see over them to Alki Point and the Sound. Now we can no longer do that because the trees are four times that height.

Originally the road reached the house uphill from Ferncliff, but as traffic on Ferncliff became heavier, the exit on our sloping road became dangerous, and we built a long, winding road through the woods that seems to be a more suitable approach to our house on the hill.

In 1973, we built a swimming pool downhill from the house. Our plan was to build a house, too, taking advantage of the view of Eagle Harbor. The pool is enclosed, surrounded by a wooden deck and has two floor-to-ceiling windows for light. Attached to the pool with a window between is a small apartment that we sometimes rent or occasionally use for a hideaway. After going through the experience of building the pool, we decided against further construction.

The immediate reason for the pool was an arthritic condition that kept me in a wheelchair. Swimming seemed to be the solution to the problem, and it was. I've swum almost daily, and arthritis no longer troubles me. We share the pool with friends and neighbors both for fun and to help defray the cost of upkeep.

Recently, I fell over the cat and broke my hip. After an operation, the surgeon said, "I didn't have to do what I did, put a ball in your hip, but if I hadn't, you would be back in another four or five years for another operation." The hip is no particular problem now.

Otherwise, I'm now in pretty fair shape except for having less energy and some creakiness due, probably, to my age.

I've decided we don't treat ourselves right. I'm just beginning to come to this. You keep hearing, "You've got to keep going; you need to be busy; activity will keep you young." Not true. Who wants to be young anyway?

I will continue to give information when I can. If I feel like it, I might write the story of the development of Winslow. I certainly have enough memories and mementos stored away to do that. Beyond those two things, I want to play bridge and learn to play pool. Mostly, I'd like to spend more time right here at home with friends I enjoy. Wilbur expects to take some trips, but I want to stay home. I love my home. It's my life. When I was very young, I preferred to stay home and not go to school; also, I loved to play. It seems I have come full circle.

Leo Clementz

Leo B. Clementz is a well-built, fine looking man of average size. Frequently he has a twinkle in his eyes which suggests amusement at himself, at someone else or possibly some inner thought. Though he is inactive now and fragile, it wasn't long ago he could be seen taking energetic walks around Winslow.

He and his wife, Dorothy, were active members of the Dona Senior Center, partially because they were long time friends of the director. They have taken part in activities at BISCC when on the island. They go to Arizona for the winters.

When the garage of the Center was being converted into an activity room, Leo's contribution, at the age of eighty-three was to pull hundreds of nails from boards to be used later for construction.

Leo Clementz

"I rolled out biscuits like piecrust and made over two hundred at a time. They were very popular with the men."

When I was born in 1901, my parents lived in a small house in the country two or three miles from a town called Marble Rock, Iowa. Our house was in the woods and isolated, with only a dirt road to connect it to town. I was born at home and for three years was an only child until a sister, Cleo, came along.

My father, Ramie, was a cement finisher. He worked with Mother's brother, Frank James. Their job was to finish off cement sidewalks and basement floors of new buildings. To do this they used trowels and spreaders with long handles called floats. It was all done by hand.

Father was short, and Mother (Clara) was tall. She was twenty-one when they were married. She was probably the typical mother for that time. Her cooking is something I remember; she spent a lot of time at it. She was strict with me, but I never minded. One of her pleasures was her church. Later, just before World War I, she was active in the Salvation Army as a warrant officer and a recruiting sergeant.

I went to a one-room school of six grades in town, walking three miles to and from school each day. Though I don't remember what we read, I enjoyed reading. I didn't read at home, but once in a while, Mother would read to us. One of my favorite subjects was handwriting. We used the Palmer Method drawing circles across the page, and my circles were round and even. I did not care for arithmetic. The teacher led us in singing at school, but we had no music at home. At recess, we played ring-aroud-the-rosy and tag in the yard and later, baseball. I was good at that and could hit home runs when some of the other kids couldn't.

Once there was a boy in front of me who had a coldsore on his lower lip. He turned around, and I stuck my pencil into his coldsore. I don't know why. He yelled, and the teacher called me up to the front of the room and spanked me. She used a strap about two feet long and four or five inches wide. It hurt. That's the only time I remember being bad in school. Actually, both at home and at school, I pretty much accepted whatever happened and didn't question. I was pretty easy to get along with.

The school sat across from the railroad tracks, and I used to watch the trains go by and wish I were the engineer.

At home, I didn't have many chores and there wasn't much to do. Sometimes, we would hire a horse and buggy at the stables nearby for three dollars a day and meet family friends in the park in town for a picnic. It was nice.

I went to Sunday school at the Baptist Church and was baptized by immersion. There was a tank in the chapel near the preacher that could be uncovered for baptisms. I remember wearing my shorts and some sort of robe and getting wet all over in front of my parents, relatives and friends. There were five or six classes in the church school, and at Christmas, we would put on a play. Once I was a shepherd and had to recite two Bible verses. My parents would go to church while I was at Sunday school. Usually after church, we had company for dinner.

I didn't go to high school though I continued to

play baseball in the community center in town. There were no youth groups at that time, but I used to take girls to the movies and occasionally to a dance. We did round dances, waltzes and fox trots. I was good at the fox trot. There was always a fine five-piece orchestra—two violins, a string bass, drums and piano. Once I took a bottle of whiskey to a dance, and the sheriff caught me and took it away from me. I've hardly had a drink since.

We moved to Billings, Montana, but then Father was offered a job on the railroad in Memphis, Tennessee. We had been there for a couple of years when Dad took me fishing. We camped by a river and I was eaten alive by mosquitoes. I had a bad case of malaria with its chills, fevers and blisters, so we returned to the more healthy climate of Billings.

In the 7X Dairy, from 2:00 a.m. to 2:00 p.m., I helped strip the cows of their milk after the machines had gotten as much milk as they could. The pint of cream I drank each day helped me to get over the malaria, along with the good water and fresh air of Billings.

As a bellboy, I ran the elevator at the Grand Hotel. A millionaire who lived there used to tip me a nickel every time I took him up to his room in the elevator.

Next to the Grand Hotel, was Burton's Candy Factory where I helped make taffy. They cooked it in big copper kettles and laid it out on marble slabs. Then when it was the right consistency, it was hung on large hooks and pulled and pulled until it became taffy.

At Elk Basin, seventy-five miles from Billings, I worked as an oiler in an oil field. There were three eight-hour shifts a day which were changed each week. The summer heat was severe, so we moved back to Billings. That's when I got the job for the railroad.

Mostly I worked in the roundhouse, a sort of garage for engines. They could be turned around to go in the opposite direction by a turntable. Once the turntable broke and I had to get in the engine and turn it manually—my dream come true. Other parts of my job were cleaning out boilers and fireboxes and re-coaling. Sometimes a fire would go out and I would have to rebuild it using kindling, then starting the blower and when it reached 200 pounds pressure, turning it off. I had the job for three or four years.

When World War I came along, I was too young to be drafted or enlist and never got involved in any way. I was never really aware there was a war.

When I was about twenty, I moved to Yakima to work in an apple warehouse owned by Richie Gilbert who had a ranch out of town. During the fall harvest, apples were brought in, sorted by machine, individually wrapped in paper that was then twisted at the top, and arranged in rows in various refrigerator cars, 756 to a car. When the season was over, we cleaned, painted, and otherwise maintained the warehouse.

Summers, I worked paving roads being built as a state highway. Once I got caught in a cave-in and was covered by dirt up to my waist. I got out all right but have had trouble with one hip ever since. I did this combination of warehouse and road jobs for eight years until the warehouse was closed because of the Depression.

Early in that period, I met Myrtle. She was a blue-eyed blonde, tall and slender—a really beautiful lady. She was a packer at the warehouse, though I really met her at a dance. In 1923, when I was twenty-two, we got married. During the following years, we had four children; Ben, Iva Dell, Bob and Jerry. Iva Dell and Leona (later) both resembled their mother. I played a lot of softball and biked, and most of the time, the family went with me.

I applied for a job as a cook at a Civilian Conservation Camp (C.C.C) during the Depression. I told them I was a cook, and they never knew any different. By trial and error, I became a good one. They used to say I was particularly good at seasoning food. There were a hundred men to feed three times a day. I had the help of a bull cook to do the preparatory work. I rolled out biscuits like pie crust and made more than two hundred at a time. They were very popular. We did all this on two huge iron ranges with ovens below, fireboxes on the side and warming ovens above.

I worked there for two or three years and then was sent with the family to cook in another camp in Port Angeles for another two or three years.

Myrtle's mother and stepfather, Harvey, lived on Whidbey Island, and we moved there looking for work. Jobs were very hard to fnd in those Depression days. I did odd jobs, whatever I could find. We found a remodelled chicken coop to live in. We gathered wood from the beach for fires. For food, we raised rabbits and had a garden, hauling seaweed from the bay for mulch; it made good fertilizer. We dug clams and made use of a community food bank. There was plenty to eat, but we had little else.

Two babies, Harold and Leona, were born on Whidbey. Leona arrived during a snowstorm, and I walked two miles in deep snow to get a doctor to come home and take care of Myrtle.

We stayed on Whidbey for about five years. Then we decided to move our family of eight to

Bainbridge Island where my parents lived in the house next to the Congregational Church. The house, in Winslow, is still there. That was in 1938. Cleo, my sister, had died at the age of thirty-five of cancer, and her six children came to live with my parents. Their father, Art McMullen, worked in Bremerton and helped out financially, but my parents raised the children, and they were a handful.

At first, Myrtle and I rented a house near the Grange Hall. Then at Pleasant Beach, we found a rental house we later bought, and it was the family home until 1975.

I got a job at Fort Ward, preparing for the war that was sure to come. During World War II, I worked in the Navy Yard helping to build boats. On order were two 220' mine-sweepers, thirteen 180' mine-sweepers, and, just after the war, seven 67' tugs. We did repair work on war-damaged ships too. They would telegraph in to the Navy yard so it would be ready for them. Some if the ships had big holes in them. Others had their bows blown off.

Jerry was in the Navy as an assistant to a chaplain. Ben was in the Merchant Marine. The other children were too young to serve.

On the island in those days, since we had no car, we walked everyplace we wanted to go. There was a little ferry from Pleasant Beach to Bremerton, but it was a mile and a half from our house to the ferry. There was a store nearby and a theater about a mile away. About once a week, we took the children to a movie. When we got there, they would run up to sit in the front rows. One night when the movie was over, we walked almost all the way home before we counted noses and realized we were minus one child. I walked back and found her asleep in the front row of the theater.

I helped build the Agate Passage bridge, completed in 1950. One of my co-workers was hurt because he got his foot caught in the loop of a rope that guided the load of a crane. He was pulled into the air and then dropped into a pile of steel. He lived, but it was rough. I went to see him in the hospital. We thought there should have been two men on the operation and that the contractor had been trying to save money by moving me to other work just before the accident.

There was a grand opening ceremony for the new bridge. The night before, Jerry and a friend walked across and back in the dark so they could say they were the first to use it. In 1952, a new road to the bridge was built—Highway 305.

Myrtle and I talked it over and decided it would be better if I found work on the island instead of returning to the Navy yard. I wouldn't earn as much, but it would be better in every other way.

McDonald School had been built on ten acres in Eagledale around the bay. It was a two-story building with a basement, and it housed six elementary grades. I was hired as caretaker or custodian. I shoveled coal—we bought ten tons at a time—fired the boilers, kept them clean and painted red. The floor was painted red too. In the fall, I raked leaves in the yard into piles the children loved to jump into. Then they would help put the leaves into wheelbarrows to take to the truck I had borrowed so I could have the leaves to fertilize my garden. Sometimes the children rode in the barrows. We all sang as we worked. Inside, I cleaned and waxed floors and stairs and varnished desks.

Then McDonald School was replaced by Blakely School, so I worked there until I retired in 1970 at the age of sixty-nine. I enjoyed the children. Sometimes at recess the teachers would ask me to watch the kids so they could do other work. and I found myself playing games and zipping stuck zippers. I had a cart on which I carried boxes filled with cartons of milk for the children's lunches. I would deliver these, and then somehow, the children would sneak out, jump on the cart, and away we'd go. Finally, the teachers put a stop to this, but it was fun while it lasted,

On February 20th, just before I retired, Myrtle died of a severe heart attack.

When I retired the following June, the parents and teachers had gotten together and gave me a present of a two-week trip to Hawaii. They made all the arrangements, even at the large hotel on the beach. Swimming, sightseeing and relaxing were such a relief from problems at home that I stayed two more weeks. While I was there, I sent some exotic flowers to the teachers back home.

After I returned, I took a much easier job. For five years, I served as janitor at the Congregational Church. I was lonely in the big house at Pleasant Beach, so I kept myself busy going to shows in Seattle, to dinners and games at the Friendship Club where I was a charter member. For Fishline-Helpline, I drove people to the doctor or shopping And I became aware of a widow, Dorothy Belling.

One day we were both at the Friendship Club. She had just missed a ride to Poulsbo, and I happened to be going there, so we drove together. She had moved into a new house in the mobile home park in Winslow and gave a housewarming to which she invited me. Later, she asked me to fix her scales. And finally, I had nerve enough to ask her to come to my house to see my collection of bottles. While we were there, Jerry called from California, and I found myself saying, "I want you to talk to my girlfriend."

Our children, my six and her four, had gone to school together. We shared friends and had many of the same activities. It seemed natural to make my girlfriend my wife. We were married by Doctor Jones at the Congregational Church on March 3, 1975. The Oakleys who lived on the corner near Dorothy, stood up with us. We moved into Dorothy's mobile home, and I finally sold the house at Pleasant Beach.

For the past few years, we have divided our time between a mobile home park named New Hope in Mesa, Arizona in winter and our home here on the island.

I am lucky to have a wife who makes music I thoroughly enjoy. She plays old-time songs and hymns on a portable electronic keyboard. I go with her when she plays at the Winslow Convalescent Center or at Chuckwagon lunches in Winslow or Suquamish.

I do have a problem with my lungs, probably due to exposure to asbestos at the Navy yard during and after the war. Breathing is difficult as I have only a thirty per cent lung capacity. Due to medication, I had a bad fall last summer and have been weakened by it and a slight heart attack last winter. I now need a wheel chair.

However, I don't complain. I've had a good life and still do, with plenty of friends and family, two good homes and a devoted wife.

INEZ THORN STORRS JACOBSEN is a compact little person with a round face and short, straight hair. She has definite opinions and shares them freely.

It would be hard to find anyone more willing and available to do a volunteer job on a moment's notice. Most often it would be serving as hostess or for the lunch program. It might also be folding newsletters, preparing for a potluck or selling tickets to a play. Whatever is needed, Inez is ready.

Inez Jacobsen

Inez Jacobsen

"The lawn was so well taken care of, it looked as if each blade of grass had a pedigree."

Mother and Father were both German. When she was eighteen, Mother came from Germany to Port Townsend and then Seattle. Father arrived in Seattle by way of Minnesota. Both were wholesome, hard-working, religious people. They did a lot of praying at our house and saw to it we all went to Sunday school and church. They were very loving. I don't remember ever being spanked or whipped, and yet they were strict. Everyone like my parents. I know I did.

Dad was well built, tall and thin. I felt that he could take care of anybody. He was a great protector. Though he was a plumber by trade, he wanted to be a farmer.

Mother looked like me, stocky with blue eyes and blond hair. Cooking was her specialty. She made all my clothes; I was probably fourteen before I ever had a store-bought coat.

When I was born in 1906, I joined my brother Percy, eighteen months older. Soon after, Mother had two more boys, Ralph and Bill. We all lived in a big house on Queen Anne Hill in Seattle. Sophie, a friend of Mother's from Germany, came to live with us and to help Mother. She became a part of the family. In the house, we had a piano, and Mother taught me how to read music. My most vivid memory, though, was the large sandbox in the back yard. It seemed to be a hangout for all the neighborhood kids who were my friends.

When I was six, we sold the house and moved to

Oregon. Dad had been fast-talked by a dentist he met into buying 400 acres, sight unseen, about twenty-five miles east of Corvallis. I think he only paid about a dollar an acre for it. But this, he thought, was his chance to farm. We travelled south in a wagon that sometimes got stuck in mud up to the axles, and I was scared. I have often wondered how Mother must have felt leaving a lovely home in Seattle for an unknown future way down in Oregon. We were met at Airlie about five miles from the "ranch." Actually we had to find rental housing at first because there was no place to live on the property. The land had hills, valleys and timber. On the part that was good for crops, we raised a large vegetable garden and wheat that needed a thrasher every year. On the farm, Dad accumulated every kind of animal, on a small scale of course. Mother had to learn how to churn butter and make bread. She never grumbled. Her health was good, which helped.

Finally, Dad built a big house on part of the land. Since he was a plumber, we were the first to have an indoor bathroom. Before starting the house, they built a barn, a big log barn. They cut the trees up on the hill, stripped the logs of bark, then slipped them down toward the site. Then the neighbors pitched in, and in two weeks, we had the barn up—a beautiful thing. It was great how the farmers traded labor. Because of this, we didn't see much money. Actually we were poor, but we didn't know it because somehow, my parents always managed little luxuries like birthday cakes and gifts.

We went to a one room school, all eight grades with about fifteen kids. When we finished grade eight, we took state exams, seated two seats apart so we wouldn't help each other. By some miracle, we passed. Then we went to high school in King's Valley, about five miles from home. We could learn at our own rate, so I thought I would try to do high school in three years. I didn't make it.

My brother and I rode a horse to school. Dad would say, "Don't run the horse." Soon as we were out of his sight, away we'd go. One day Percy got a cart somewhere and hitched the horse to it. We were going to school in style that day. But the horse wouldn't move. He was used to running as one of a team, and he simply wouldn't move by himself. Percy lit a fire under him. Still he wouldn't budge. He just lay down on top of the fire. He was scorched, but he was okay. I was crying because, although I trusted my big brother, this somehow didn't seem quite right.

Another time, we were left in charge, and a goat got sick. "He's constipated," my brother said, "He needs an enema. Go get Mother's enema bag. I did, and he took care of the goat. He really did. It looked like there was more of the goat outside than in. The next day the goat was dead; it had died in the night. I had cleaned and returned the enema bag so Mother never knew what happened.

When I was about ten, we took a trip to Newport on the ocean. Neighbors in a buggy kept pace with us. Actually, we kids walked most of the way because the wagons were so slow. We slept out or under the wagon at night. Meals were food we had brought from home; there were no restaurants. It took the better part of a week to get to the coast. Mother developed pneumonia in Newport, and we had to go home.

A few years later, she had two more babies, Dorothy and Helen. I was a built-in babysitter which, along with my high school studies, kept me pretty busy.

Christmas was an important event at our house. The big deal was packages from Seattle. Mother had two brothers and two sisters in Seattle, and Dad's father had married twice and had nineteen children. They probably all felt sorry for us way off in the wilderness and so were generous, sending food, clothing and sometimes toys. Mother knitted and crocheted mittens, scarves and sweaters for gifts. In Germany, all little girls learned to knit by the time they were eight, so she'd been knitting for a long time. Dad dressed up as Santa, and my little sisters believed he really was Santa even when they discovered Dad was always missing when Santa arrived. They just never put two and two together. My toys were all right, but a cousin nearby was an only child and had much better toys, so I played with her whenever I could.

Each year we went to the state fair in Salem. Dad rented a cart for four dollars, and a friend took all six of us. We each had a dollar to spend.

I'm sure the years we spent in Oregon taught us a feeling of responsibility. We all had chores to do, and we learned how to help each other.

When I was sixteen, our relatives insisted we move back to Seattle. Dad decided that although he enjoyed farming, he could make more money plumbing. I wanted the big city and a better school. Mother was eager to return to her family.

I started to go to Lincoln High School, but because I'd been attending a one room school and didn't have enough credits, they put me in freshman classes. I said, "To heck with this. I'm going to quit school and go to work." I got a housekeeping job. Dad was trying to feed eight, so I gave most of my money to Mother to help out.

My employer wasn't very nice to me. She rode me pretty hard and criticized a lot. Her son-in-law, Mr. Yeaman, befriended me and introduced me to Mr. Slattery who owned apartment houses on Capital Hill. He hired me as a telephone operator in one of his apartment buildings. While I was there, I took a comptometer course and went to business college and got pretty good at shorthand and typing. I quit the telephone job and went to work at Western Electric as a secretary. Then I heard about an opening as telephone operator on the *Ruth Alexander,* one of three passenger ships that travelled between Seattle and southern California. It sounded like fun, which it was.

It took a week each way. There were three stewardesses and three telephone operators. I was the youngest. I earned $45 a month plus my uniforms and medical and dental care. I loved that job. I had dates in every port and good friends in San Francisco who took me out to dinner and to musical shows. There were dances every night aboard ship. We weren't supposed to go, but when there was a masquerade, we went anyway. We had third call for dinner, but there was always plenty of food. The stewardesses sort of looked after me. So did Paul Storrs, the third mate. He was very handsome, slender with blond curly hair and blue eyes. He visited me at the switchboard and kept an eye on me otherwise. There was some drinking among the crew. It didn't mean anything to me. I just thought it was funny when a stewardess tried to put a canary, cage and all, through a porthole or when she sewed all her roommate's stockings together at the top. Paul said he thought I was having too many dates and really should get off the ship. After seven trips, I did. Besides, I couldn't wait to drag Paul home to meet my mother and father.

We got married in 1927. Jack, our son, was born in 1928. I went back to work, this time as head of the order department at Carnation where I stayed for twenty-five years. A full time housekeeper made this possible. Paul joined the fire department and worked his way up to pilot on a fire boat.

In 1948, while he was still with the fire department, Pope and Talbot divided some Gamble Bay property, and we bought two lots. We lived in a quonset hut while we were building our home on the beach with its daylight basement and cement bulkhead. Oysters and clams were plentiful and seagulls busied themselves catching searun cutthroats. I saw one seagull out on the beach struggling with a fish almost too big for it to handle, so I ran out and took the fish away from the seagull. That night, we had it for dinner. Pleasure boats anchored out in the bay in front of our house weekends. Occasionally, a friend in a fishing boat would whistle, and I would go down and get the lovely salmon he had saved for us. We lived there for eighteen years, even ten years after Paul retired in 1955.

Every May and September, Paul and I used to go to Reno to play the machines. Sometimes we won, sometimes we lost, but it was always fun, and a trip to look forward to.

The last time I went gambling was with a friend, Helen. We took a three-day trip to Cactus Pete's place in Jackpot, Idaho on the Idaho-Nevada border. I love that beautiful country. I was playing the two dollar machine when a security guard stopped by and said, "Stick with this machine. It's a good one. You're going to hit it." Suddenly bells clanged, and 800 dollars came spewing out of the machine onto the floor. I think that's my last gambling safari, though, because I get too tired, and on the bus, my feet swell.

Jack grew up, went to the University of Washington and got a degree in meteorology. Later when he was working at the weather bureau on Tatoosh Island, he met Edna, a nurse from North Dakota whom he married. They gave us four grandchildren.

In 1965, Paul had a heart attack and spent fifteen days at Harrison Hospital. He was never very well after that. He had a ruptured appendix and an aneurysm. For the last five years of his life, he required constant care, as he often passed out. When, in 1976, he died of cardiac arrest, it was a release for him and a relief for me.

We had moved to Bainbridge and there I took up bowling. I wasn't on a team, just a substitute. A male team needed a fourth member. They were told I was available but I was a woman. They said all they cared was that I could bowl. So I joined the team. One of the members was Jake Jacobsen. He and I started seeing each other apart from bowling but made it very clear that he didn't intend to marry again and I didn't intend to give up my firemen's pension for anyone. Well, we changed our minds, and I'm glad we did. I was seventy-one and he was seventy-nine.

Before we got married, I insisted on a prenuptial agreement because I wanted to be sure his three children would inherit his property, which they had enjoyed with their mother. And he wanted to be sure I would be financially secure if anything happened to him. His children accepted me like one of their own. They still do.

We lived a problem-free life in his lovely home

54

on Agate Point—no troubles with children, no financial worries, plenty of household help. Mostly we played in the yard, gardening. It was some garden. He raised every kind of flower except roses. His specialty was rhododendrons for which he won blue ribbons. Starting in May each year, people would come from miles around to look at his rhodies. The Rhododendron Society made him its president one year. The lawn was so well cared for, it looked like every blade of grass had a pedigree. Jake had the respect of everyone on the island. If he needed help of any kind, he would call someone who would be there in no time.

After we'd been married only twenty-three months, his heart gave out. That day he had mowed the whole lawn then climbed up the outside ladders of the two cement tanks up on the hill that provided water for his garden. It was too much. I called 911, but it was too late. He died the next day. He was eighty-one.

His children said I could stay in the house as long as I liked, but it was far too large for me to care for alone. I moved to a small apartment in Winslow where it was central enough so I could give my car to a grandson. They wanted me to take anything I wanted from the house, and I took a coffee table and some other furniture which will be returned to them when I no longer need it.

I learned a lot being associated and living with Jake. He was such a loving, caring, compassionate person. Those twenty-three months were the frosting on the cake. Of course, when I was very young and met Paul, I thought he had hung the stars and the moon.

Now the days go by fast. I still substitute for bowling, sometimes on a moment's notice. Jake had been pleased that I joined the Bethany Lutheran Church. Its FFF (Footloose and Fancy Free) group of older people meet once a month for a potluck and I attend that and also church on Sunday. The American Legion Ladies' Auxiliary helps various organizations and recently bought $900 worth of gifts for patients at the veterans' hospital in Retsil. I helped wrap these gifts. I belong to Bainbridge Senior Center and am often called to serve as hostess or for the Chuckwagon lunch program. Recently, I took eight tennis lessons and was the only one to finish the course.

My health is very good. What have I got? Nothing. I thought I had arthritis in one knee, but it went away. Sometimes when I am searching for a name, it escapes me, but if I forget about it, it will come back later.

I guess if you ask me what is most important to me right now, I would say that because of the good life I've led, and still do, and because of Jake's influence, my strongest desire is to do something nice for somebody every day, some one thing to help someone. It might make the person feel a little better. It might bring a little happiness to someone where not much is going on in his or her life. Some people just need a listening ear.

Fanny Nerup

FANNY BATES NERUP is a small woman whose white curly hair always looks as if she has just left the beauty parlor. The few wrinkles on her fine skin serve rather as decorations than as evidence of age. Blue eyes, often unobstructed by glasses, shine with humor and with love.

She served Chuckwagon lunches at the Dona Center for two years and sang alto in the Omega Chorus for fours years. She is a member of Bainbridge Senior Center although no longer active except to bake pies and cookies when needed.

On her eighty-fifth birthday, she was given a party at BISCC, and she told some of her life story which inspired the following personal history.

Fanny Nerup

"We needed a man with a gun to escort us to school because hungry wolves came into town in packs."

In 1904, when I was two, Mother took me from our home in Lancaster, England to Gloucester for a three week visit with her sister, Emma. At the end of the visit, Mother returned home, but she left me with Aunt Emma and Uncle Albert with whom I lived for seven and a half years. Why she did this I never knew for sure. Later I didn't ask her because I figured that if she wanted me to know, she would have told me. But I could guess. I was the last of eleven children, eight girls and three boys, and a very late baby. Father was seventy-six and Mother forty-eight when I was born.

I enjoyed my years with my aunt, uncle, and four boy cousins: Jim, Bill, Tom and Albert—all grown up. All the men were miners. It seemed like every man in those days was a miner. They must have doted on me and treated me like a beloved daughter because, though I never owned a doll, never had a Christmas tree, never had a birthday party, I was a happy child and felt special. They called me "Fannyoann."

We lived up on Viney Hill. There was no fence around our place, so we had a view of the valley below. In summer, gypsies would enter the valley in their brightly colored wagons. They would park and set up their tents. They would come up to the house to sell things—handmade lace and other items they had made. I would go down and play with the children. Some people say gypsies steal little girls, but that wasn't true as far as I know. I even ate with them. They were good people. They had carnivals. I loved the black pea soup they sold. And if you want your fortune told, go to gypsies. They are good at that. They told my Mother that she would take a long trip to another country and advised her against it. It was good advice as we discovered later. But you had to be careful about letting them into the house or even the yard, because they would steal anything they could get their hands on.

In front of the house was a stone well, our only source of water. It was round and about seven or eight feet across and rose four feet from the ground. It was gorgeous. Nearby was what we would call a patio with chairs for relaxing. I don't remember what kind of flowers there were, but I do remember pink, yellow, blue and purple blossoms. Gloucester is in the southern midlands of England and has a climate like that of southern California. We spent a lot of time in the yard. I used to sit outside by the hour while my aunt combed and brushed my heavy, waist-long hair, dark with auburn streaks.

The house was built of stones and had a thatched roof. Inside, the floors were flagstones about three by four feet in size. When they were scrubbed with pumice stone, on hands and knees, they were snowy white. There were no carpets. We cooked on an open fire. There were ovens on either side of the fireplace. We pulled our chairs up to the fire to keep warm.

When Uncle Albert could manage, he bowled on outdoor bowling greens. He got to be very good, and entered tournaments in nearby towns. Once he entered a bowling match in Cardiff, Wales which wasn't very far away. While he was there, he found another mining job, and when I was five, we moved to Cardiff.

I started school there, a very large school it seemed to me. It had an exercise yard, and on Tuesdays and Thursdays, the entire student body would do military training exercises outdoors. We girls were dressed in white middy blouses and dark blue pleated skirts.

Inside was one big room where we all gathered each morning and at the end of the day for prayers. Sliding glass doors formed classrooms. We were separated by grade, and boys and girls were taught in different rooms. On Mondays and Wednesdays, we girls would knit khaki wool socks and scarves for the military. On Fridays we could bring anything we wanted to knit or sew. I usually brought a dress to hem or a blouse I was working on. I learned to make all my own clothes, and I never had a sewing machine. I got rewards for good penmanship, but I lost them later in my travels.

When I was nine and a half, Mother called to ask my aunt to bring me home. My father was ill and not expected to live very long. He spent his time in bed or in a wheelchair. I felt it was my duty to keep my father company, that he needed me. All my older sisters except Ethel had married and left home, though most of them lived in town. Flora, a younger sister, who, I learned much later, was really a niece, was five years old. Two brothers had died in infancy. The other brother had been killed in a coal mining accident while I was at my aunt's. He had been working in the pits pushing a coal wagon when a metal piece on the bottom of his clog came loose, got caught in the wagon and pulled it over on top of him. He was eighteen.

None of us wore shoes—only on Sunday. We wore clogs. They had handsome leather tops and iron cleats on the heel and toe so they wouldn't wear out. You could wear them forever.

For six months after I returned home, Papa and I got acquainted. Because I had been in Wales for five years, I spoke mostly Welsh. My aunt had to translate many of our conversations. As I remember him, papa was short and heavy-set. He told me many stories about his twenty-one years in the British army. He had served in the Crimean and Boer Wars. He had been stationed in India for many years. Toward the end of his career, he became a member of the Palace Guard in London and wore his famous busby hat with pride. He retired with honors in 1869 at the age of forty-three. I still have the retirement papers and medal he received at that time.

After his army duty, he became a miner, and that's how he supported his large family.

Papa had a remedy for stomachache. He would ask for senna tea which I learned later was a strong cathartic. Then we would dip toast into the tea. We called them "sops." Sops were supposed to cure the pain.

He loved black and white peppermint candy he called humbugs and would send me to the store to buy it for us. I couldn't speak English, but I could point to the humbugs.

His tiny sister, Margaret, came to visit him once a week. She would sneak a bottle of rum in the large pocket of her skirt. Mother would have disapproved, but Papa was used to rum because in the army a noggin of rum was a daily treat no matter where he was. I used to laugh at Papa and his sister. Of course I didn't know what it was all about, only that it was a game.

Papa died in 1912 at the age of eighty-six. He was buried in a military cemetery with full military honors including the Union Jack and six horses to draw the casket.

After Father died, Mother decided to go to Canada to join a daughter and her husband, Eliza and Lewellyn, who lived in Stewart, British Columbia, a gold-mining town. Eliza said in a letter, "Mother, I think you can do better here. I know you're having a hard time making a living for Fanny and Flora in England. Just sell everything and come here." They sent us tickets and money to make the trip and scheduled us to take the *Titanic* in April. However, Flora became ill with pneumonia, so we cancelled our reservation. When we heard that the *Titanic* had sunk on April fifteenth, we remembered what the gypsy fortune teller had said. Finally on Friday, June twelfth, we sailed from Liverpool on the *Empress of Britain,* leaving behind two sisters, Margaret and Emmy.

When we reached the open seas of the Atlantic, I was seasick and stayed that way for five days. On Wednesday the ship slowed down and everyone went on deck to find out why. They discovered the ship weaving its way carefully among icebergs. Some people were reminded of the fate of the Titanic and were uncomfortable, but I was fascinated. To my surprise, the icebergs were blue, not white. And the shapes! I imagined I saw cathedrals, animals, towns. They were magnificent.

We arrived in Quebec on Friday and stayed just long enough to make preparations for the train trip across Canada. We were told we would need our own food to cook on a stove at one end of the train carriage. And we would need our bedding. I can still see the blue enamel container with handles at each end that we carried our blankets in. Occasionally we would be able to get off the train to buy fresh food and goodies and to stretch our legs.

We slept on the wooden seats we used during the day, by pulling out shelves from underneath the seats. Then we wrapped up in our blankets. It was a tiresome week-long journey to Vancouver, B.C.

After a few hours in Vancouver, we boarded a ship for Prince Rupert where we landed a day before Dominion Day, July first. Three days of patriotic celebration and parades later, we boarded another ship to take us to the head of the Portland Canal and the town of Stewart. The Portland Inlet and Canal, about ninety miles long, takes off from Chatham Sound fifteen miles north of Prince Rupert and about one hundred fifty miles south of Ketchikan. It flows almost due west.

On the way, we stopped off at Simpson where the workers and townspeople were Indians, to drop off supplies at the cannery. The captain took us to see an Indian burial site. Natives buried their dead not in the ground but wrapped in blankets and, surrounded by their possessions, up in the trees. No one could stay there very long because of the smell.

When we arrived at Stewart, we had to wait until the tide came in to tie up at the mile-and-a-half long dock. In town, narrow because two mountains loomed above not far from the shore, walks and houses on stilts were built ten or twelve feet off the ground because when the tide came in, the town was flooded. If we wanted to cross the street, we had to row. When the tide was high, I kept falling off the walks. I just wasn't used to them. In summer there were about 1500 people; many moved away during the winter. Mother found work in the home of Judge Conway, where she cleaned and cooked. We lived in town above what used to be a drug store.

Flora and I started to school. I was in the fifth

grade. At first it was hard because I now not only had the Welsh and English languages to deal with but the Canadian dialect as well. In spring and fall, classes were held in a large school out of town, but they were held in a church in town in winter when twenty-four feet of snow fell, and the temperature was seventeen degrees below zero. The frozen snow was so deep we had to go out the upstairs windows to walk on top of it. We needed a man with a gun to escort us to school because hungry wolves came into town in packs. At night they would howl outside our windows.

For fun, the people took out the windows in an unused store and flooded the floor to make a skating rink. And of course there were sleighs and sleds.

When the weather warmed, ice from the glaciers above in the mountains, broke off and rolled into the river with a big splash. The mine was opened, and trains began to take ore from it to place on barges which would deliver it to a smelter.

In summer, we wandered out of town to Alice Arm, a small inlet where the Kitsault River emptied, and we would pan for gold, brought down by glacier water—not seriously but just for fun. I caught my first salmon in the river. We crossed the Canada-Alaska border to shop in Portland City, now Hydar, leaving the boat on the Canadian side. When we bought anything, we had to go through Customs on the dock before returning.

Later that summer, I moved to Anyoc on the American side with Eliza and Lewellyn. A copper smelter was being built there, and Lewellyn and his father were hired to build houses for the workers. For a few months we lived in a tent on the beach about a mile and a half from town. Then we moved to town to live in another tent, this time with a wooden floor. There were 3,000 men in camp living in tents while they waited for houses to be built; the tents were very close together. For a while, except for my younger niece, I was the only little white girl in town.

Then my sister, Eliza, had a premature baby which wasn't expected to live. She sent for Mother who came to help her, bringing Flora and Ethel. We all lived together in the tent until the house was finished. Mother's care which included daily dips into a warm mustard bath kept the baby alive. He lived until the age of seventy-two.

Mother found work with a doctor as a midwife, which kept her busy as the town grew. There was no hospital.

Then an old friend convinced Lewellyn that he could make a better living in Ketchikan, Alaska, so he and his father went while the rest of us worked for months to earn enough money, $350 apiece, to enter Ketchikan. We also needed our boat fare. We worked hard doing any kind of work we could find: child care, cooking, laundry, cleaning. There was no school in Anyoc so I could spend all my time working. I was twelve. Finally we took a ship to Ketchikan. We arrived on March 17, 1913. On March twenty-seventh, I would be thirteen years old. We showed our money at Customs and went ashore.

And that's when we got to Alaska; and that's *how* we got to Alaska.

Ketchikan is a long narrow town spread along Tongass Narrows. It is on a mountainous island named Revillagigedo and is separated from the Pacific Ocean by some small islands and the larger Prince of Wales Island. The weather was rainy or, in winter, very cold, but I didn't think very much about it when I was young. Later I hated it.

66

When we arrived, the town had about 1,500 people, most of them connected with the fishing business. The day we got there, we found a room in the Stedman Hotel which still exists. At night we went to a St. Patrick's Day dance at the Hippodrome. I had learned to dance at school—even the Highland Fling.

We lived in Ketchikan for thirty-nine years. First we lived on the beach about a mile and a half out of town on Charcoal Point. The area had been homesteaded, which accounted for the settlement there. To get to town and to school, we had to row and landed at Ryus Dock. Eventually a narrow road was built connecting the Point with Ketchikan. Logs formed the base of the road and planks were placed on top of them. It was very rough. Also a school was later built on Charcoal Point.

There were no canneries at Ketchikan when we got there, only the New England Cold Storage, but there was one on the mainland across Clarence Straits at Kasaan Bay. Mother, Ethel and I went there to work the summer I was fourteen. We worked eighteen hours a day, seven days a week and earned twenty-five cents an hour. It was barely enough to live on, so we picked berries when we could. I had to work so hard I couldn't do the things a young girl would like to do, like dance. It wasn't very exciting, and I got so tired, all I could do when I got home was fall asleep.

Daily, salmon were caught in traps and brailed or lifted into scows to take to the cannery. There they were thrown into chutes which led to a floor from which fish were beheaded, slit open and slimed or cleaned by a machine called the Iron Chink which had replaced the Chinese laborers who had formerly done the job. I learned to do all the different tasks in the cannery.

Mother developed fish poisoning from helping with the sliming. She had 150 boils on one arm from wrist to elbow and she was in great pain. When the *Mariposa* came to pick up the canned salmon, Mother went aboard to go see a doctor in Ketchikan. It took six months for her to recover from the infection. Ethel and I stayed until the summer was over. We needed the money, and every little bit helped.

The following winter, Ethel met and married a man who built fish traps. There were 150 fish traps in southeast Alaska at that time. Ethel and her new husband moved to Newtown Hill, and I would go stay overnight once in a while. Her husband was drowned a year later and she moved to Prince Rupert. There she met and married a man named Charles Gundery. Eliza couldn't stand the dampness, so she and her family moved inland to Alberta. We never saw much of her after that. Mother, Flora and I were now on our own, so I cleaned houses after school to help my mother. She was not feeling well because she had a goiter. She finally let one of the three doctors for whom she worked, Dr. Meyers, operate. Her medical care wasn't satisfactory since there was no hospital in town at the time, so the operation left her weak the rest of her life.

She did get the contract to clean the new Charcoal Point School, but I had to do most of the work. Every morning I went early to build the fire. Then, if it was snowing, I would make a trail so the children could get to school. I attended school myself as much as possible and finished the eighth grade. After that, I had to work full time to support the family.

Housework in those days was different from

can-can. We had Prohibition so there was no drinking. I remember one officer in particular, an engineer named Jimmy Jefferson, because he introduced me to my husband-to-be at a dance on October 16, 1917.

Charles Nerup was five feet ten inches tall, slender, very good looking and sixteen years older than I. He was Norwegian and had lived at the home of the Norwegian consul in San Francisco while adjusting to the United States. He liked his job with the Lighthouse Service in San Francisco and didn't want to leave. But he was assigned to a new ship, the *Cedar*, as first officer and sent to Ketchikan. The *Cedar* arrived at night in the pouring rain and had to anchor out. More than anything, Charles wanted to turn around and go back to San Francisco. Then we met and began going together, and he felt different. By February, he was ready to go to Juneau, the state capital, to take his exams for both captain's license and American citizenship. He took one, and he wanted to take the other the next day, but it was a holiday. However, he told Judge Bell, "I've got to take this exam today. I have to get back to Ketchikan."

"What's your hurry? Do you have a girl there? If so, who is she?"

"Yes, I do, and her name is Fanny Bates."

"Oh I know her. She's a fine girl," said the judge. "All right, let's do it today."

When Charles got back to Ketchikan, he proposed. That was in February. On October 16, 1918, exactly a year from the day we had met, we were married.

At first we had a small house. Then we decided to build, and we built on top of and around the house we were living in. For foundation, we used what it is today. We had to carry our water from the creek. Then to heat the water, we had to build a fire for which we brought in the wood. For cleaning, everyone made his own soap. I used whatever was provided. To wash clothes, we first boiled them in a copper kettle to loosen the dirt. We lifted them with wooden paddles into a big tub on a bench where we scrubbed them on a corrugated washboard. Then we rinsed them in another tub, wringing them out by hand one by one, and hung them up to dry. To iron the clothes, we sprinkled them individually and rolled them up to distribute the dampness. Then we heated on the stove the heavy pointed iron. When the iron was hot, we attached the handle and ironed while another iron was heating on the stove. For cleaning floors, Mother made me knee pads. Sometimes I used a cushion. You'd think I'd have arthritis in my knees, but I don't.

For a while in the winter I worked in the woods as a whistle punk with the Heath family. My job was to pull the rope that rang a whistle to warn men to get out of the way because a donkey engine about a half a mile away was starting to haul some logs. It was these logs which were used to build the first highway from Charcoal Point to Ketchikan.

On the way home, I passed the Lighthouse Service of the Territory of Alaska. The station was on a corner on the way to Charcoal Point, and I often saw in passing, the fellows who worked on the tenders that serviced the buoys and lighthouses as far north as the Bering Sea and the Pribiloff Islands. I also met the young men at parties at the station. Hostesses would leave a message for me at the store that I was needed to help at a banquet or a dance. There were other dances when ships came in. I loved to dance the fox trot, the tango, even the galvanized water tanks placed in the ground and filled with cement. Charles was gone a lot, so he would show me how to plaster, sand and paint, and I would do it while he was working. I even shingled the roof. It turned out to be a beautiful home.

We needed the additional space as Flora and Mother were still with us and would be for seventeen years. Besides, our own children started coming a year after we were married. One was born every year or two until 1927. The first two were girls, Inga Elizabeth and Thelma. Then a ten and a half pound boy, William, was born. A caul, a thin membrane, covered his head and face. Of course, it was removed, and he still has it preserved in a glass jar. After that, two girls, Flora and Fanny, arrived, then one more boy, John Howard. By that time, I was twenty-five. Ten years later, we had another son, Robert, who lives now on Bainbridge Island.

Just before William was born, I had a psychic experience which was new to me, though I have had many since. I was wide awake, but I saw a vision, a man in a long white robe with a halo. He said "Don't worry. You are perfectly all right. I will be with you always." I have seen him and talked to him many times since. He is my guardian. He is the spirit of my husband's grandfather who was a minister. Once I saw him standing behind our pastor as he was preaching. He always looks the same. I can ask him anything. It's easy to do, but I don't do it very often. I see lots of things through him I could tell people, but I will not tell them.

Other people have guardians too. If a person would listen, he could hear his guardian and ask him questions, but people don't listen.

I too am a guardian, though I am still alive. My son is a pilot on a ship, and he knows my spirit is

71

with him on the bridge of that ship. If I'm not there, my husband is. Bob knows he is safe.

As the children grew, we had a lot of fun and many parties at the house. Every holiday was reason for a party. Being housebound when the weather was freezing was another reason. All the neighbors came to our house. I would serve hot scones with butter laid in and hot chocolate. The girls would dress up in my clothes. Inga would play the piano, and everyone would dance; dancing felt good on a cold winter night. They would make up pantomimes. We all loved music. When Charles was home, he would sometimes take his guitar, which he played by ear, out back of the house, and John Howard would stand on a stump and yodel to the music. We were one happy bunch. Charles was full of the devil. He had a bag of tricks picked up in his travels. One he got from a magician was to tie me up in a gunny sack and refuse to let me out. What the children didn't know was that I had a stick inside and I knew how to let myself out. They puzzled for a long time over that one.

On Christmas Eve, the children would go to church, and when they came back, one or both of us would have set up the tree and hidden the presents back of the piano and in other secret places. Then we would have our Christmas.

Instead of going out on Halloween, we had a party at the house, partly because of an experience I'd had as a girl of fourteen or fifteen. About ten girls and several boys went out for trick or treat. They had a bobbin attached to a string that made a loud squeak when dragged across a window. One Finnish lady was so frightened that her husband and another man chased us clear into the woods. I said to myself, "If I ever get out of this, I'll never play tricks on Halloween again." And I never did. So we had our parties at home while other kids were laying things on the new road so cars couldn't pass. We dressed up as ghosts and witches and played games. We didn't bob for apples. I never heard about that until we got to Seattle much later.

Charles and I never quarreled. We had differences of opinion but usually worked them out. I would never argue. I would walk away from an argument or I would listen and keep my mouth shut. I still do. Charles had his ship, and I had the house. I raised the children, although when he was home, he did guide the boys. He wasn't home much. For twenty-five years, he left in May and returned in November. When he was about to leave in May, he would say, "Now boys, your mother has to have wood so she can cook for you and keep you warm. You must bring it in every night, enough for the next day. That's an order." And they did it. I handled the girls and had no trouble with them either. I really enjoyed my children.

Of course we had our problems. All the children except John Howard, had the usual children's diseases which, with seven children, meant quite a few sick beds. Generally, though, they were healthy, for which we were grateful.

We had one bad period when Thelma and Mother were in the hospital at the same time. The two older girls were leaving to go on a Girl Scout camping trip when Thelma was run over by a car which dragged her fifty feet along the road. She had to wear a silver plate the length of her leg for some time. When she came home, I set up a bed on the glassed-in veranda. Charles who had come home on emergency leave to help out, consulted a bone specialist in Sitka. He suggested that Thelma roll a

73

bottle several times a day with the bottoms of her feet. She never did limp.

Mother was terminally ill. I spent as much time with her as I could while Charles managed the household including two nieces who were visiting. Mother was in a great deal of pain. I think it was diabetes. I know it had something to do with her spine. She never left the hospital and died there in 1927 at the age of sixty-nine. I missed her. We had lived together throughout many pretty rough years.

Since supply ships rarely came to Ketchikan in winter, we had to can food when it was fresh. We picked and canned berries, fruit, cranberries and also canned meat. On the return trip from Westward—that's what they called the area that extended out to the Pribiloff Islands and the Bering Sea—the men would hunt and bring home deer meat and sometimes caribou. Once a friend gave us bear meat. We canned it all. There were no fresh fruits or vegetables during the winter except a few from Canada which were very expensive.

No food came in packages. We bought oatmeal in big sacks. When it was cooked we called it mush. It took 100 pounds of flour a month to make enough bread, pies and cake for my family. The first packaged food I remember was a Pillsbury cake mix. To promote it, the grocer gave away large decorated pink plates. My son-in-law in Seattle still has mine.

The fishing industry was in trouble because the traps were luring all the fish, so the seiners and Indians couldn't compete. The seiners would try to catch fish in the creeks, or they would make deals with the men at the traps and pirate fish away from them. Charles sailed the *Cedar* to Seattle to pick up Interior Secretaries Redfield and Bell who came from

74

Washington, D.C. to Alaska to investigate the situation. As an end result of their findings, creeks can no longer be fished, and instead of year-round fishing, there are special seasons. There is only one fish trap left in Alaska now, and it is off Cape Chacon on the southern tip of Prince of Wales Island. It belongs to the Annette Packing Company.

Ketchikan began to grow. Several canneries including the Sunny Port Cannery and the New England Packing Company were built, as was a spruce mill. In town there was a new Federal Building. The high school burned down, but was replaced by a new one. The city grew north to include Charcoal Point which developed into a large residential town and shopping mall. Austin Towers, a large condominium, was built.

South of town, a new highway connected Ketchikan with the New England Packing Company. The Lighthouse Service became a part of the Coast Guard which built new headquarters five miles south of town at Indian Point.

About a mile and a half south of Ketchikan, the red light district grew up. I still say if they had those houses now, we wouldn't have the problems we have today. The girls were pretty isolated. They came to town once a week with a chaperone to shop and go to the doctor who did his best to prevent disease. Otherwise, they stayed in their houses and entertained men from Ketchikan and fishermen who were away from their homes for months at a time. It's nature, you know, and they had nowhere else to go. I approve of that arrangement. Some Ketchikan business men got rich on those houses.

During those years, I began to go to see mediums. One of them once told me, "Fanny, you have more power than I do, but you don't work it.

You have a halo around your head constantly. Whoever it is in the other world really takes care of you."

I did and do sense when something unusual is happening, or going to happen. Once my husband's ship was towing a scow loaded with cement for building beacons near Sitka, Alaska. The scow leaked and sank. At that moment, I had terrible stomach cramps. I called the wife of one of the officers and said, "Something's happened. Charles has gone down in the water." I discovered later that he had, but only to investigate. He was safe.

I learned to pray to ask for something and would receive it within an hour. Sometimes I get lonely for my children and say, "Oh how I wish I could see my daughter," and the phone will ring and Flora will invite me to spend the weekend with her in Kent, mainly to just talk, which means a lot.

I learned to conduct seances myself. They're fine. I can work the table, but you have to have people who are not afraid and who believe. I don't do it often because I don't know people who want to. You have to be good spirit people, and there should be someone who can pull me out of a trance if I can't.

Once in Ketchikan, Mrs. Balcom asked if I would have a seance for her. She'd been so good to me, helping with transportation when I wanted to pick berries and had no car. So I said, "Of course, if you want to." She brought some friends, and we began. "Oh my gosh!" I said, "We've got people here we shouldn't have. They have no business here. The table will go crazy if we don't watch out." And the table picked right up off the floor. Those people weren't afraid, but they were evil. I won't work a ouija board because they are evil too.

During World War II, Charles, on the *Cedar,*

was stationed in the Aleutians which were being bombed daily by the Japanese. We didn't see him for two and a half years. There was great fear of invasion. William too was in the army in the Aleutians. John Howard was in the Merchant Marines. Of course we worried about them constantly.

The war years were full of danger in Ketchikan too. Resident Japanese were rounded up and interned. We had blackouts when no lights were permitted at night in or out of Ketchikan. We all had gas masks, even the children. I kept mine until we left Ketchikan in 1953.

Charles brought the Aleuts and some Eskimos out of the Aleutians to Ketchikan where they were put up in barracks at Ward's Cove Lake. He also piloted ships delivering American troops to the Aleutians from Annette Island. Once he piloted a mammoth oil tanker on its way to the Westward from Cape Chacon, through Nichols Passage, between two islands and into Ketchikan. He was chosen for these special piloting jobs because he knew the country and its waters so well. After all, he'd been sailing them since 1917. Later he was appointed commander at the base. He retired after the war in 1948 at the age of 62 after serving for thirty-four years and six months.

After Charles retired, we lived in Ketchikan for a few years, but it was getting too expensive, so we decided to move to Seattle. We were attracted too by a warmer climate. We sold our home, and with fourteen-year old Robert, we sailed to Seattle. For a week we stayed with our married daughter Inga. Then we spent another week at the Claremont Hotel. By then we had found our home on Queen Anne Hill—a four bedroom house on McGraw Street five blocks from Queen Anne High School.

We were lucky to become part of a small community where the neighbors all helped one another. The Robbins lived on one side of us, the Brooks on the other. A widow lived across the street and a police chief nearby. We were like a big family.

The next few years would probably sound dull to anyone who didn't live them. Charles said he would never go to the waterfront to see a ship again and he would never wear a white shirt. He spent his time growing the most beautiful garden on Queen Anne Hill. He planted dahlias, begonias, gladiolas and especially roses. There was a gravenstein apple tree in the back yard that produced enough apples to feed the whole neighborhood. Charles puttered around the house completely replacing the plumbing system among other things, while I kept in touch with the family and prepared Sunday dinners each week for them.

Bob graduated from Queen Anne High School in 1955 then went to Washington State University for a year. He signed up for the U.S. Navy and went to boot camp in San Diego. After a Christmas in Alaska with his family, he went to officers' school and graduated from there to active service in the Navy. We were left to live alone.

In 1968, Thelma died of cancer at the Virginia Mason Hospital. Her body was returned to her husband in Ketchikan.

Charles had been ill for some time. He had several prostate operations. He had malaria attacks from time to time—a disease he had picked up in Panama when he was young. Then he developed Parkinson's disease. For years he was in and out of the Marine Hospital. The children knew nothing about it until one day Inga saw him with the shakes. Later when she was visiting, we heard a thump in the basement and discovered Charles had fallen and hit the back of his head on the concrete. Mr. Robbins came over and took him to the hospital. Mr. Robbins called Flo who came to stay with me. Charles had to be moved to Harborview because the Marine Hospital lacked the equipment necessary for the operation on the back of his head. Robert came home from Washington, D.C. He stood by his father's bed in full uniform waiting for his father to wake up and recognize him, which he did. But soon he started rambling on about Ketchikan; he was delirious. He went into a coma and never came out of it. He died on January 6, 1974 at the age of eighty-eight. He had suffered a great deal, but always tried not to put it on me. Doctors had been told not to give me details of his condition. He thought he was protecting me.

Inga succumbed to cancer in 1978. I was visiting Bob in Washington and I wondered why I hadn't heard from her. She was trying to prevent my knowing she had bone cancer.

John Howard brought his retarded son to Seattle to be examined at the Children's Orthopedic Hospital. He was diagnosed as slow. He is very musical and spends much of his time listening to records from his collection which numbers into the hundreds. After the exam, John Howard took his family back to Alaska. I never saw him again. He left on Tuesday. On Thursday, Flo called to say he had been killed while handling and lifting merchanise of the company for which he was manager. Some boxes had fallen on top of him. I was reminded of the time a neighbor of my son in Alaska told my fortune by numbers, somehow connecting numbers to the letters of my name. "I don't do this much, Fanny," he said, "but I'll do it for you and

John Howard." He told me I would have an illness but not bad and that I would live to be 102. Then, after looking at John Howard's numbers, he refused to tell him his fate. That was shortly before John Howard was killed.

In 1975, about a year after Charles died, Bob had a tour of duty as executive officer of a ship stationed on the coast of Italy. I went to visit him and stayed for six weeks and enjoyed every minute of it.

Seventy-five of us navy people visited Florence. My companions were the chaplain's wife and the wife of the supply officer. It cost $75 a week and we had a hotel room with continental breakfast.

The many cathedrals we saw were beautiful with much gold decoration but were musty and dirty; they really needed cleaning.

Once a gentleman put his arm around my shoulders. "Why did he do that?" I asked.

"That means he loves you," I was told.

"Sorry about that," I said.

On the buses we were served wine. I was warned not to drink the water, and I don't like soft drinks, so wine was what I drank. We even went to a monastery to see how it was made. It tasted good in Italy, but I haven't had any since.

Another side trip took us to Rome and St. Peter's. We saw the dark catacombs below with its tiny little cells, and on the main floor, the finely carved crypts. At one point we were told to look up, and we saw a large painting of Jesus with a beard, and another nearby of Jesus without a beard.

As we left the Cathedral, the Father who was our guide said, "Hold hands until you get to the bus so I won't lose you." It was Holy Week. The Pope was about to speak in the square and thousands of people were pushing and crowding to reach a spot where they could see and hear him.

While I was in Italy, Victor, a neighbor, wanted to ask me some questions. I told him we would need a seance to find the answers. I asked Bob, my son, and Penny, his wife, to sit with us. Penny was afraid and nervous, but we set up the card table anyway. I said, "If there is one knock in answer to your question, it means the answer is no. If there are two, the answer is yes. First we need a true spirit. We must pray." Victor wanted to speak to the spirit of his dead father. We got him. "You don't have to ask your questions aloud," I said. "Fanny, I'm not afraid to say anything in front of you," said Victor. So he asked his father why, many years ago, he had left Italy to go to the United States where later Victor was born. The answer was one knock meaning no, his father did not wish to answer. As a medium, I could converse with the spirit. I asked why he didn't want to answer his son's question. The spirit of the father said, "He's a good boy, and I don't want to tell him." I said, "Victor, let it go. Your father is happy. Just let it go."

Then Victor asked if he should marry his wealthy girl friend and the answer was one knock or no.

At that point, Penny became so nervous she felt ill, and we had to stop.

Many years later, Bob learned Victor had married the girl, he was very unhappy and eventually divorced.

The same year I planned a trip to Ketchikan for Christmas. I went down town in Seattle to buy Christmas presents. While I was waiting for a #4 bus across from the Post Office on Union Street, a pane of glass fell from a window above and hit the back of my head. There was no blood, so though I was still covered with glass, I got on the bus and took my packages home. Then I walked over to see my doctor who called Flora to come and get me to take me home and put me to bed, but to awaken me every hour. He was worried about a concussion. In the morning I felt fine, but when I combed my hair, it all came off the back of my head. It had been cut off by the glass. We laughed about that. My head must have been bruised or the nerves injured because once in a while ever since then I get an ache in that spot.

Then Bob, who had served twenty-five years in the U.S. Navy, was transferred to Bremerton as executive officer of the *Sacramento*. He heard of the school system on Bainbridge Island, and he wanted a good education for his four children. Three boys have graduated from Bainbridge High School, and a girl still home will be a senior next year.

Bob built a home on the island, and I helped him build it. It included an apartment for me. I sold my Queen Anne house and moved to Bainbridge in 1977. I lived with Bob and Penny for two years and then moved to my own apartment at the Eagle's Nest, where I stayed until January of this year, when I moved into the new Finch Place Apartments.

Each year I have gone to Alaska to visit my sons, one son now. I joined the Dona Senior Center and served lunches there for a couple of years. I went to the Catholic Church for mass every morning at 9:00 until recently. It's too far to walk now. I sang for four years in the Omega Senior Chorus and wish it were still going. And I have many friends.

Every summer I go to Yakima to visit Fanny, to Pascoe to see John Howard's widow, to Alaska where William still lives, and I frequently see Flora, whose home is in Kent. She usually drives me to see the other girls.

You know, I'm a very happy woman. A doctor recently told me I was unusually healthy for my age. I said, "Of course; I'm happy, and if you're happy, you don't have anything to worry about." And I'm in good shape now, although a year ago, I did have a heart attack. I began to perspire and got weak and wanted to vomit all the time. Finally the sixteen stairs down to the laundry were too much for me. After ten days of intensive care at Harrison Hospital, I got well fast. I had good nurses who kidded a lot. One asked me if I wanted a man or a woman for a roommate. For a while, I thought she meant it. There was one man nurse who was a riot. When I left the hospital, I stayed with Bob then Flora for a month and then went home and haven't had a sign of a problem since. Of course I walk a lot. I get two other women in the apartment house to walk with me.

While walking home from Thriftway the other day, my right knee went out. I managed to get home with the help of a neighbor, then passed out. Someone called 911. That's the knee I injured when I was fourteen slipping off a log backward while picking berries. I had to miss a planned trip to La Conner and a cruise.

I still want to go there some time, and there are some other places I want to go. Charles helped build the Panama Canal, and I'd like to go through it on a ship—and into the Caribbean. I've never been through the Wrangell Narrows either. Charles was responsible for installing that very intricate set of lights and buoys that guide boaters through those treacherous narrows. Also I'd like to see Petersburg, Alaska. I've already signed up for a trip to Lake Louise this coming October.

I was once told by a medium, and I believe her,

that I would live to be 102 years old. Since I'm only 85 now, I'll have plenty of time to fulfill my dreams, as well as to watch develop the lives of my four remaining children, sixteen grandchildren, and twenty-four great grandchildren.

Arnold Abbeal

ARNOLD CONLEE ABBEAL is a tall, slender man with erect posture. He has fine, dark gray hair and wears glasses. His contribution to Bainbridge Senior Center has been a term of two years on the board of directors and the important work of helping to shingle the new 25-by-55-foot addition to the building. He is unable to take an active part now but drops in frequently with Margaret, his wife.

❧ Arnold Abbeal ❧

"If you're a small boy, and you're sitting there doing nothing, you're going to do something. I was always in the doghouse for doing whatever little boys did."

My happiest childhood memory is of going camping with my parents and another couple to Loon Lake about twenty-five miles north of Spokane where we lived. We drove in a buckboard drawn by a team of horses. It took a day and a half to get there. We slept out on the way. When we got there, we'd put up a tent and set up housekeeping. When it rained, the grownups would play pinochle, but I didn't have anything to do. If you're a small boy, and you're sitting there doing nothing, you're going to do *something*. It seemed whatever I did would get me into trouble. But most of the time it was sunny, and we could play ball or go fishing. I loved the freedom and being outdoors.

Dad was a six-foot, bald-headed man who looked like Tom Landry, coach of the Dallas Cowboys, when he stood on the sidelines with his hat on. I thought Dad was great because he taught me how to play ball and took me fishing. By trade, he was a contractor, carpenter and builder.

I remember Mother as a tyrant because she punished me for running away by making me stay home. I ran away often because I wanted to do something, see someone. It was lonely at home as I had no brothers or sisters. A brother had died before I was born in 1906. I was always in the doghouse for doing whatever little boys did.

I got into trouble too at Marcus Whitman

Elementary School, where John Rogers High School now stands. We would stand behind a stack of cordwood sixty feet long and twenty feet high and throw rocks over it at the school building.

When I got caught, the teacher would put me under her desk where she usually kept her feet. There was one teacher I liked in grade school. Her name was Miss Wiseman. She always had a smile, and she was always fair.

The only subject I was any good at was math—except for manual training which we took at Hamilton School two miles away. In the shop, we made footstools, library tables, and those little ironing boards for sleeves. We did lathe work, and I still have around someplace a nutbowl I made then. I worked with my Dad too doing carpentry. In fact, I had my very own tool set.

When weather was good, we played baseball. Most of the boys lived within three or four blocks. In winter, adults flooded the valley below and made a skating rink where we played hockey. We sledded down the hill beside the school and down another hill called Little Baldy east of the Hilliard district where the Great Northern Railroad terminal had its machine shops and built boxcars—now a part of Burlington.

I sang with the Whitney Boy's Chorus, a community group of sometimes 3,000 boys from all over the city, directed by Mr. Whitney, a gray-haired man with a goatee. We sang concerts in auditoriums and parks, and once some of us took a train trip to perform. On that trip, one of the boys opened a coach window and jumped out. We were still at the terminal waiting until the train was fully loaded. Apparently, he had fallen asleep and was dreaming about his paper route. He started to wake up, and while he was still half asleep, he dove out the window so he could deliver his papers. He was injured, but not killed.

Fourteen of us graduated from grade school and went on to North Central High School. There's a new building there now. Five years ago when it was built, we had a reunion, and bricks from the old school were sold for a dollar apiece.

I didn't like high school and did as little work as possible. My worst subject was English—conjugating verbs and grammar. I tried to read *A Tale of Two Cities* but never could get past the first two pages. I did read westerns.

What I liked was sports—especially baseball and basketball. For four years I was on the swim team doing the 100 yard crawl, free style and lost only one race. The Y.M.C.A. had after-school gym classes three days a week and a basketball league. Those were fun.

While in high school, I served as counselor in a Y.M.C.A. summer camp. There were six cottages with six boys to a cottage. In the morning, I would get the boys up, lead calisthenics and flag raising, and the day began. Bill Becker, another counselor and I also served as life guards.

Later, one of the best jobs I ever had was as life guard at the city swimming pool in Spokane. We worked eight hours a day sitting up on our perches watching the swimmers. Four times daily, we had to get in the water ourselves and swim to keep in practice. We got two dollars an hour which was pretty good pay in 1923.

Another job I did for pin money was ushering at the Pantages Theater from 6:00 to 11:00 seven nights a week and at Sunday matinees. You see, I didn't have much time to study, even if I'd wanted to.

In grade school, boys and girls played together sometimes; we rode our bikes on Sundays. Then in high school, the girls' aquatic team provided girlfriends I could take to movies and dances where we did the fox trot, and always for the last dance, the waltz.

After graduation in 1924, I got a job as machinist in the Hilliard shops, since I'd been playing on the Hilliard team. Then the coach at Whitworth College talked me into going to college on scholarship to play basketball and in the spring, baseball. It was something to do.

A friend of mine on the Hilliard team suggested I go to Pullman and encouraged me to join the Sigma Phi Epsilon fraternity. I had a four-year swimming buddy whose sister I had dated. She was working in the book repair shop at Spokane. One day, she phoned and said, "I have a job for you over here at Pullman waiting tables and doing dishes in a sorority house." I told my boss, Alex Campbell about it, and he said, "Okay, I'll see you next summer." The sorority was kitty-corner from the frat house. I worked with a big Norwegian kid. We set tables, served the girls and then ate our own meals in the kitchen—the best part of the job. I was playing basketball and attending classes at the same time.

A fraternity brother who lived in Wenatchee encouraged me to join the City League baseball team there. It was a semi-pro team that played other cities. I worked at Morris Hardware, a not too satisfactory job, but jobs were hard to find in 1927.

One Saturday night, I went to an outdoor dance at the fair at Levenworth. The dancing was done on a four-foot platform built over a meadow. There I met Margaret Crofoot, an attractive dark curly-haired girl of seventeen. She was finishing up high school. Her mother's illness had kept her out of school caring for two young sisters, and she was working to complete her high school course in three years. Actually, we only met that night. Later we got better acquainted at the regular Saturday night dances at the Odd Fellows Hall.

We started dating, and in November, 1928, we were married in the Leavenworth Methodist Church in front of her family and our friends with a fraternity brother of mine as my attendant. Few people fussed about weddings in those days; too many couldn't afford them. I didn't invite my parents because I figured *I* was doing the marrying. Besides, Dad was involved with his activities and Mother, who would have trouble with her only son marrying at all, would have wanted to manage the whole deal if she had come.

We honeymooned in Seattle because, through Margaret's sister, I'd gotten a job there. Seattle was installing new street lights on First to Fifth Avenues, at Eastlake and down First South. They were bronze poles on a base and had three lights. I worked all winter in 1929, right after the stock market crash, in eight inches of snow much of the time. There were fifty on the crew, but I was the only one who would show up the mornings after deep nightly snow. I hauled streetlight bases on a cutback touring car with a flatbed, from the foundry to the warehouse south of where Sears Roebuck now stands.

We lived on Lake Dell Avenue in the Leschi district in an apartment upstairs in a house. We went to a lot of movies at the Blue Mouse Theater, I remember. We had no car, so we had to take a bus, street car or the Yesler cable car when we went anyplace.

The Seattle street job came to and end. The ballteam at Morris Hardware in Wenatchee wanted me to return there so I could play baseball. Fortunately, a job at the hardware store was a part of the deal. For fun, Margaret and I went fishing at Lake Wenatchee and spent much of our recreation time playing bridge all night with the Gregs, Art and Flossie, a friend of Margaret's from Cashmere.

In 1930, it was tough in Wenatchee, as everywhere else in country. One Saturday, we came back from skiing on a friend's hill at Stevens Pass to get my salary check, and discovered it had been cut in half. To further cut the boss's expenses, three of us took turns taking a week off without pay.

My brother-in-law had a two-ton truck with which he was hauling workers to the east end of the Great Northern eight-mile tunnel being built near Merit. He had an idea. "Why don't you take my truck the week you're not working, pick up coal at Roslyn, a Northern Pacific owned coal mine, and sell it at Wenatchee?" So I did. I bought four tons of coal at a time for three dollars a ton and sold it for ten dollars a ton. I had to shovel the coal off the truck by hand through a small basement window and then clean up the mess. It was hard work, but we never went hungry. We had no chains on the truck, but the weight carried us on. Of course when you stopped, you might have trouble starting again. Trucks in those days had no defrosters. I would place three candles on the dashboard, and that did the trick.

Then I had a chance to work at a quarry at Charleston just out of Bremerton. Rock from the quarry would be broken up, then passed through a grating to a rock-crusher below, where it was placed on a conveyer belt that took it to the bay. Then it was loaded into barges. My job was to keep the pulleys of the conveyer belt greased and also to help load the barges. Then the barges would be towed to Hood Canal and unloaded on shore in stockpiles as big as a house. Rock was lifted by an iron contraption called a clamshell that could pick up 4 yards of crushed rock at a time.

We men lived in the bunkhouse, and there was a commissary between the highway and the bay. The quarry boss had a rackety hotel in Sultan, and he gave Margaret and another girl jobs there "managing" the hotel. There must have been at least three customers during the entire summer.

In July, one of the barges caught fire due to the carelessness of a crew member, and in five minutes, the whole thing was ablaze because the cables were full of grease. A tugboat turned the barge loose out in the water until it burned itself out.

That job came to and end. Meanwhile, I had bought a 1928 Pontiac roadster. It was a bear. It had wood-spoke wheels that squeaked when the weather was dry in summer. In 1931, we headed for Spokane, but going through Wenatchee, we saw Morris, and he reminded me it was baseball season, so there I was at the hardware store again.

And once more, I just wasn't making enough to live on, so we drove to Spokane hoping for something better. I noticed Consolidated Freightways had a depot on Division Street across the Spokane River, so I went there and talked to the foreman. When he asked me what I had done, I told him and then added, "and I've played baseball." He said he'd seen me play and gave me a job. There were thirteen of us, and we would wait around for a loaded truck and trailer to come in. Then we took turns unloading. While we were waiting, we played penny ante poker. I made more money playing cards than I did working for an average of a dollar a day. One of the drivers who delivered the freight to town got a job at the Spokane Flouring Mills, and I took his truck and began working steady for forty-five cents an hour. What a break! At the end of the month, the boss would say, "How much cash do you really need for rent, food, etc.?" Then he would give us that amount in cash and the rest in company stock.

Consolidated began building its own terminals and warehouses. It built one on Pacific and Sheridan that had a full basement. At sheep-shearing time in Montana, the basement would be full of burlap sacks of wool, eight feet high and three feet in diameter. Then trucks would haul it to Portland, Oregon to refine. We handled 10,000 bales of wool in a year.

In 1936, Consoliated transferred me to Seattle where I loaded freight on the docks. I got tired of that and started driving on the road again. Trucking was big business during World War II. In fact, I was exempted from military service because of it. We would haul fifteen loads a night between Seattle and San Francisco, changing drivers every 200 miles for eight hours in a relay system. We hauled eight inch shells, life rafts ten feet wide that took three pilot cars to get them through, torpedoes from Keyport and deck guns for tankers. We had to be especially careful not to pick up riders, because we needed to concentrate on what we were doing and could afford no distractions.

Margaret was working as a volunteer at Air Interceptor Command which had its headquarters in the King County Building in Seattle. Each small town had eight to fifteen people working to observe plane activity and report it to the command post where all air activity was plotted on a big board. Margaret wore a khaki dress uniform. One day, Mrs. Roosevelt who had come to Seattle to see her daughter, Anna, visited the installation and pinned Margaret's Air Force Wings on her.

One of the best periods in my life was when the children were little in Seattle. I enjoyed raising kids. It seems they grew up far too fast. Four 12-by-14-inch photographs on our hallway wall show what good-looking children they were and still are. Daniel, born in 1940, just before the war, is now single, following a brief marriage. He started out to be a mortician but is now a chiropractor in Los Angeles. He managed to spend some time in the Air Force at Hickam Field in Hawaii. Marian is three years younger. After college, she taught school, then married and has two children. They live on Bainbridge Island where she has returned to teaching as a substitute. We are very proud of our children and Marian's children.

At Consolidated, we used to be one big happy family. Then after the war, things started getting tough. One dispatcher couldn't give an order without swearing. Another would let me sit for sixteen hours plus my eight hour layover time out of town—very poor scheduling. I finally couldn't take the problems any longer and quit, gave up my pension and everything.

I probably would have felt pretty let down about it all, except that in Spokane, Dad was sick and needed help. He had several rental apartment buildings that needed attention. So we went back to Spokane. He died a week after we got there. Mother was still alive though, and I continued helping her for a while.

Two jobbers, Burroughs and Lambert, handled wholesale tobacco and candies. I bought from them and set up a route that took about a week to cover and sold their products. There were thirty-five such routes handled by individuals. I figured one year I had bought $300,000 worth of tobacco and candy. We didn't make much though, only about one percent on the tobacco and five percent on the candy. I did this from 1951 to 1954, headquartering in Moscow, Idaho.

Previously I had a problem with a sacroiliac nerve, and one day it hit me again while driving the candy wagon. I had twisted myself picking up a box of Milky Ways. I could not press the clutch and could barely get out of the car. It seemed wiser not to drive any more, so I sold the wagon.

I took the proceeds from that and some other money and bought a soda fountain where we also sold hamburgers and doughnuts we made in the basement. One Monday in 1960, I ran across the street to get change at the bank. Then I ran back and put the money in the cash register, but my right hand didn't work right. It felt funny. I walked about fifteen feet over to the sink, grabbed hold and collapsed. A dentist having lunch in the restaurant came in and had a hard time prying my hand loose, but he did, then laid me on the fur coat of a customer, spotted Dr. Wilson on the street and called the ambulance which took me to the hospital and an oxygen tent. I'd had a stroke at age fifty-four. That was the first week in December. On Christmas Eve, I was home again.

That night, the soda fountain and doughnut shop, as well as the barber shop and jeweler's nearby burned down. The building that housed the jeweler's shop was a very old one. He had left a night light on, and apparently there was a short in the wiring. Our equipment was insured but, though it was carefully maintained, it was 20 to 30 years old, so we took a rooking.

I was pretty angry about the whole situation, but I knew my first responsibility was to get well. Our basement steps had a one inch galvanized pipe hand-railing on each side. I spent three or four hours every day going up and down those steps. By spring, I could play golf but not very well. I never worked again except at minor jobs like doorman at the Elks Club.

In the meantime, Margaret went to work at the hospital as a receptionist. Then the girl who did the medical records asked for Margaret's help and later suggested she take a correspondence course. She became a medical records librarian by mail, took some extra college courses and continued doing this work until 1974.

We moved from Moscow to Poulsbo in 1975, Margaret to be near her sister and I to enjoy the fishing in Puget Sound. We set up our mobile home in the Seabird Mobile Court.

My son-in-law worked with Nob Koura in Seattle. Nob was involved with the Meadowmeer Golf Club on Bainbridge, which in 1977 or so was building a clubhouse. Equipment and tools were disappearing so we agreed to move our mobile home onto the site. We could play all the golf we wanted, and my health improved somewhat. After four years, the club needed the space to build a garage for golf carts, so we had to move.

The next eight years, we lived in a series of apartments ending up in Winslow Arms where we have a cozy place that looks out through french doors to a green lawn and some woods beyond.

Health is a problem. My vision has deteriorated to not being able to read or watch television. Cataracts were the beginning of the condition. I use the radio a lot, especially KIRO's Bruce Williams' *Nettalk* at night and any kind of sports during the day. Going out for dinner is no longer a treat, as I can't see the food because most restaurants are so dark. Fortunately, Margaret is a good cook. She's quite a girl in fact and has been for the sixty years we have been married.

If my leg were better, I would do a lot of walking, but it's stiff, won't bend. A bypass from the artery of one leg to the clogged artery of the other saved the leg, such as it is. I have learned recently that my heart is slightly enlarged, and I have high blood pressure which is being treated by medication.

Now I'm living life day by day and letting time take its course.

Ruth Watkins

RUTH ANDERSON WATKINS is a tiny woman with a flashing smile, dark hair and a large amount of energy. She has recently adopted Bainbridge Island with enthusiasm as her permanent home. Faithfully, each Tuesday and Wednesday, she serves lunches at the Center. The Bridge Club also counts on her presence each week.

Ruth Watkins ❦

"We did everything together. We even had two vacuum cleaners and two lawn mowers."

I live alone in a small gray house with a blue door. A tiny plot of green grass separates the house from a paved road that leads to the post office and shops in Winslow. In the house I can have hot water, heat, light, clean clothes, refrigeration and telephone communication on demand. My Thunderbird sits in the driveway outside. All these conveniences leave me time and energy to do whatever I want to do. I have choices.

That was not always so in my life. I was born January 27, 1907 and lived my early years on a 160 acre farm in a small farming community near Elgin in eastern Nebraska. Farming and housekeeping were hard work in those days. Farmers needed help. This may have been one reason for large families. I was the third of eight children, six girls and then finally, two boys. Even though most of us were girls, we all worked. We didn't resent hard work or question it. We just took it in stride.

Of course, my parents needed other help too. Mama always had a hired girl to help her in the house. Papa had at least one hired man and often two or three. Then during harvesting, shearing or moving stock, we might have four or five. I remember one tall, good-looking hired man we had. He was probably in his thirties. He wanted to get married but couldn't find anyone nearby, so he advertised for a wife in I think it was the Omaha paper. A girl answered and they started a correspondence. After a while, he left and brought back his mail-order bride. For some reason, he didn't seem very happy about it; he didn't talk or anything. We couldn't understand it because she seemed nice enough. Papa finally asked him what the trouble was. The hired man told him his wife was at least three months pregnant. The poor man was embarrassed and disappointed. Within a few weeks, he took his wife and left. They moved to Kansas, and we never heard from them again.

The farm produced wheat, corn, alfalfa, cattle, chickens, sheep and hogs. And we had teams of horses. We had a huge vegetable garden, an orchard and Mother even had a flower garden. It seemed we worked as much outdoors as in.

My sisters, Myrtle and Carrie, used to work with me to pull rye from the wheat. We sometimes argued about who had done the most. Myrtle once got her leg cut with a jackknife, and I always thought I had thrown it at her in anger. My conscience bothered me for years. Later when we were reminiscing, she said she had cut herself. This is not the only time I discovered sisters do not always remember their childhood in the same way.

We picked corn when it was ripe, throwing the ears into a wagon pulled by a team of horses that walked up and down between the rows. We worked alongside hired men. It was just a part of life.

When harvest time came, the grain was cut and tied into bundles in one operation by a machine that dropped the bundles as it went along. Then six or eight were shocked or placed in teepee form with the grain at the top so it could dry. We girls would help with this. Then the Baumgardner men, some German neighbors, came with their thresher. The straw was spewn into a stack on the ground, and the grain into a wagon and taken to storage sheds and even-

102

tually to a mill.

The Baumgardners were accustomed to a mid-morning and a mid-afternoon lunch, dinner at noon and supper at night. This was a lot of work for my mother even though she had the help of the hired girl, her daughters and neighbor women who took turns.

Besides crops, there were animals to care for. Our cattle, beautiful white-faced Herefords, pastured during the day, but in the evening they moseyed back to the stockyard where they were fed grain or whatever. Pigs in a pen we gave grain and what we called slop, leftovers from the kitchen. I was permitted to feed the pigs but not the cattle.

Our sheep were fed on Grandfather's farm three or four miles away. Two of us girls would herd the sheep each day. We had a good dog named Shep to help us. To keep them from straying, we had to watch them all day, though I don't remember seeing a coyote, from which we were protecting them. Toward evening, we herded them into a pen. Then the two of us rode home on our pony. By that time it was getting dark and scary. I don't remember much about shearing the sheep, but I know we did it. Of course for nine months in the winter, we went to school at the Park Center community school and only worked after school.

When it came time to sell the cattle or sheep, they were driven into Elgin about ten miles away. I used to help, walking along behind, but when I got tired, I could ride in the wagon. It was always fun to go into town. We could look forward to Papa's giving us pennies to spend.

We had chickens and milk cows. I could gather the eggs, but I could never milk a cow. I couldn't make the milk come out. That made my sisters mad because they thought I was trying to get out of work. Pails of milk were brought into the house. Some milk was used for drinking and used in cooking. The rest was separated, run through a machine that divided the milk from the cream. After the cream soured, we churned it into butter.

We had several teams of horses. The matched grays were especially pretty. They were all dear to us. A couple of work horses would let us ride them, as well as the several riding horses. Papa surprised us one day with a Shetland pony, Robin. He was white with a few brown spots. Papa even got a buggy for him. We loved that pony; he was our friend.

My parents, Daniel and Laura, were both born in Iowa, and according to my memory and photographs, were good looking. Mama's distinguishing feature when I was young was dark hair so long she could sit on it. She wore it in braids around her head. Her parents died when she was young and her grandparents raised her. In college she lived with eight girls, whose lives together seemed like one big party. She decided a large family would be fun. Whenever we argued or caused trouble, she would say, "This is not the way I planned it."

Dad was not very tall and had a mustache and by the time he was forty, his hair had receded. He was always kind. When he went to town, we could count on his bringing us a present even if it were only a piece of candy. Almost every time he went any place, he took one or more of us with him. Papa's family of parents, four boys and a girl, had decided to homestead in Nebraska. When they got there and were unloading the wagon, his younger brother, while taking out the shotgun, shot and killed himself. He might have been saved if Dr. Peterson, summoned from ten miles away, hadn't delayed in order to finish his dinner.

Our house was situated back from the road with a large cottonwood tree in front that had a swing in it and two similar trees in back. The house had three bedrooms upstairs and a huge kitchen and living room downstairs. In the kitchen was an outsize table where we ate and a Majestic coal and wood range that also burned corncobs. The stove had a warming oven above the cooking area, a baking oven and a boiler on back for heating water. The living room had a heating stove, and there was a potbellied stove upstairs. I don't remember ever being cold.

We had no indoor plumbing. A three-holer with its Sears Roebuck catalogs sat in the back yard apart from the house. It was the delight of boys and even men to tip it over on Hallowe'en. The windmill and water storage tank were close to the house, and pipes from the tank ran out to the stockyard. We got our water from the well by using a hand pump. Butter, milk and cream were hung down the well to keep them cool since we had no refrigeration. Every year Mama canned four hundred quarts of apples and cherries from the orchard, vegetables from the garden, gooseberries and currents. All of it was stored in the cyclone cellar, a large underground room built out by the windmill. The room was fortified for safety and the floor covered with hard-packed dirt. Double doors horizontal to the ground opened out. Inside the room were shelves on each side, eight to ten feet high, and at each end, bins for apples, carrots, potatoes and turnips.

We were quite self-sustaining except for flour, sugar and such. Papa butchered pork and beef as we needed it. When he did, we might have choice loin chops for supper that night, and Mama cooked the heart and tongue the next day.

Outside the house, Mama's flower garden was fenced in by red lath. Inside the enclosure grew the flowers she loved including lilacs. I used to go out there and sit in the quiet. The front yard was so large it had to be mowed by a team of horses. A grove of ash trees on the north side of the house became an occasional playground. Myrtle, Carrie and I used to play house there for hours, marking off rooms and using orange crates for furniture.

Our telephone hung on the wall and worked with a crank. It seemed like everyone in the community used the same line. Each phone had its own ring, like one long and two shorts. We had no radio or television, so when someone had news, he or she rang five long rings, and everyone got on the line to hear the latest. We three girls had voices that sounded alike over the telephone, so we deliberately confused people when they called, as a form of entertainment.

Years after we moved away, a cyclone passed through the area, uprooted the big cottonwoods and destroyed most of the buildings. I never saw our home and farm after the cyclone.

The farming community that surrounded us was called Park Center. Park Center people were strict in their behavior. We could play cards but not with a poker deck—only card games like Finch, Bingo, Old Maid and Pig. Gambling of any kind or drinking liquor were frowned upon, and dancing. Square dancing was popular, but it wasn't called a "dance."

Papa was active in this community. He was influential in building a playground near the church that had a basketball court, baseball field, horseshoe posts and playground equipment. We had community picnics there too. Each family brought its dinner and laid it out on a long table and everyone helped himself. The Tills ran a cattle ranch and had their own ice house and smoke house. They always brought home-cured ham that was the most delicious meat ever.

Papa worked hard to get a new school built in Park Center. During my first year in school, we studied in a one room building. When he was campaigning for state aid, he put a picture of us five girls in the Omaha paper. We were all dressed up in white sailor suits and stood in stairstep formation from the oldest to the youngest—Sybil, Myrtle, Ruth, Carrie and Beth. The caption under the picture read, "Five Good Reasons Why Mr. Anderson Wants a High School." We got the money and built the first country high school in Nebraska. There were two classrooms, one for grades one through six and the other for grades seven through ten, with a hall and office in between. Pupils came from some of the other rural schools to get their first two years of high school. What I remember best about my ninth grade class was the boy in front of me who sat there and killed flies with his hands, picked them up and put them on my desk. He was good at it too. I thought he was repulsive, but I didn't say anything.

Everyone said the Anderson girls could not sing. I guess the reason was that we really couldn't sing. I took piano lessons but never accomplished much. One thing we could and did do was "speak a piece." Papa was our teacher, and a thorough teacher he was. He taught us to speak loud enough and slowly enough so everyone could hear us. At school and church programs, one of the Anderson sisters usually spoke a piece. When I was about twelve years old, I did this for the last time at Thanksgiving. Because I thought I was too old, I hadn't learned my lines, but the teacher made me do it anyway. I had to be prompted every other word. I swore I'd never do it again, and I never did.

What a job it must have been for Mama to get six girls and two boys ready to go to the Congregational Church on Sundays and to keep us quiet while we were there. The sermons were often long. I know Mr. Clifton kept us from 11:00 to 2:00 o'clock many times.

Our family had a country store near the schoolhouse about three quarters of a mile from home. We girls helped run it, filling in shelves, waiting on customers, candling eggs and snitching bananas, chocolate cookies or cheese. At that time, bananas came in big bunches hung from a hook. Once in a while there would be a tarantula among the fruit. Oranges, lemons and grapefruit came individually wrapped in off-white tissue paper and boxed in crates. I collected the Sunkist coupons until I had enough to get a set of grapefruit spoons.

I remember our first car. Here came Papa one day driving up to the house. I don't recall what make it was, but it was a two-seater that had a top made of canvas on a frame that could be lowered or raised. Later we had a Model T.

We had the usual childhood diseases. The one I remember most vividly was measles. We all had it at the same time, and some of us were very sick and had to be moved down to the living room to be near Mama during the day. Dr. Peterson came and gave Mama a bottle of medicine. No matter what the ailment was, he seemed to give us the same medicine out of the same bottle. One time he came to vaccinate us for small pox. I had ridden a horse to the store for something and hurried home so as not to be late. I was so nervous by the time I got home that after I slid off the horse and got my shot, I fainted.

During World War I, my father was active in war work. He had something to do with the Home Guards. He also was head of sugar rationing for the area. He told us about how people in the community felt about boys who didn't go to war; often someone would paint yellow streaks on their mailboxes or barn doors.

Just after the war ended, the Spanish Influenza epidemic swept the country, supposedly brought home by the soldiers. Papa went down to Missouri to see about some land an uncle had bought, and he came home violently ill with the flu. He died within a few days. There was no funeral parlor in Park Center. When a person died, the body was kept at home until the funeral, and someone sat with it at night. Because of the seriousness of the disease, the funeral could not be held in the church, so it was held in our front yard. I was eleven years old.

I had never known death before. I couldn't believe my father was gone and I would never see him again, the man who was always there to smooth away our sorrows, to take his son, Lyle, out to the barn to see the horses and cattle. I could express my grief only by crying. I cried all the way to the cemetary until Mama put her arms around me.

We had to go on, to adjust to the painful circumstances. We were not wealthy, but we certainly had plenty. Mother was left with eight children to feed, clothe and educate. She and Papa had long ago decided we would all have an education. We sold the store to Grandpa and Uncle Charlie. At a big sale, we sold our precious teams of horses, the farm machinery—everything. Albert Kinney, a neighbor and relative, agreed to rent the farmland on shares.

When Sybil graduated from high school and started teaching four or five miles from home, we bought a Model T Ford. That was when I began to drive. I don't remember ever learning. I just got in the car and drove. We probably didn't go much over fifteen miles an hour. My job was to crank the old Model T because I thought I was the one with the knack.

We drove into Elgin to a picture show once in a while. The night we went to see *Black Beauty,* it rained. At that time, all roads were dirt, and the dirt throughout that area was clay that got heavy and sticky when wet. We had a terrible time getting home in the dark of night. We got stuck, and all of us had to get out and push.

After I finished tenth grade at Park Center School, I went to Elgin for my junior and senior years. Three of us girls from Park Center had an apartment together. We took turns by the week cooking, bringing most of the food from home. I liked high school in Elgin. I was on the basketball team, had parts in the junior and senior plays, helped with the junior-senior banquet in the spring and went ice skating and to dancing parties.

Because there was no college nearby, Mama decided we must sell the farm and move to Chadron, a college town in western Nebraska. The banker, who was the villain in our lives, had swindled Mama out of considerable money, but we had enough to make the move and to make a down payment on a three-story house near the campus. It had been owned by a woman who took in roomers and boarders. Mother continued with this so we could go to college. We all had our own rooms and were expected to care for them ourselves. Also we were expected to help with the gardening and cooking.

I graduated from high school with a teaching certificate since I'd taken a teachers' training course. I got a job teaching in a rural school district near the small town of Hay Springs—the first in my class to find work. The salary was unusually high, ninety dollars a month for nine months. My good fortune was probably due to the fact that it was difficult to find anyone who would teach in that particular district which was ten miles out in the country. I was eighteen years old.

There were three members on the school board. At first, I stayed in the home of the president. I thought it was the awfullest place I had ever seen. Animals roamed around at will in the front yard and even up and down an indoor hallway. I didn't stay there very long.

Next I stayed with a family in a comfortable house with indoor plumbing and french doors between the living and dining rooms. Every afternoon when I got home from school, Mrs. Walgren was baking a cake. We ate it for supper, and I usually found a piece in my lunchbox the next day. They had a horse I could ride when I wanted to. I remember one foggy morning I went for a ride. When I started to go home, I kept trying to turn the horse in one direction, but he insisted on the other. As it turned out, he was right.

My school had one room and about a dozen students, and I hated every minute of the time I spent there. I think now that what was really bothering me was that I was homesick. At the end of the month, I was issued a warrant, a receipt for having taught, instead of a check. It had to be signed by each member of the school board, and I had to go to each one to have that done. Then the warrant was as good as a check.

At that time, in the 1920s, there wasn't much for a girl to do except be a teacher or a nurse. I didn't want to nurse, but had to work. Maybe teaching in town would be better. After a stint in Hay Springs where I had eight students and liked teaching better, I moved on to Rushville where, for four years I taught grade six. That was more interesting. The children had their basic skills down pat and were ready to do many challenging things. Carrie came to Rushville, and we had an apartment together and had a lot of fun because the town was larger and had a lot more to offer. Mama kept house for us in the roomy upstairs apartment while selling the house in Chadron. Lawrence joined us too, and that was a wonderful year.

I had been going with Hollis Lintt for two or three years. We had met at Chadron State College. After college, he taught junior high in a nearby town and felt he was ready to marry. The bank where he had his money had failed, as many banks at that time were doing, so he had no money, but he did have a job. My bank had not failed, so I had a little money which was good because I knew I would not be able to teach after I was married. School boards just wouldn't hire married women. We weren't worried in the least. Everything was going to be just fine. So in 1934, we went to Hot Springs, South Dakota to get married—all by ourselves. Hollis was a stubborn man and refused to marry at home, and I went along with his idea.

Hollis wasn't making enough to live on, so we decided to go to Worland, Wyoming to go into business with his sister and her husband. I don't know why we thought he would be able to get along with his sister. He never had before. The partnership lasted about five weeks.

We hadn't had a honeymoon. This seemed to be a good time for it, so we took a trip through Yellowstone National Park—camping, fishing and mountian climbing.

Hollis had another sister in Denver. We went there to try our luck with a gas station. Brother Lyle came over from Chadron to help. The station was a complete flop; there were no customers.

Hollis tried everything, even selling Hoover vacuum cleaners door to door. Finally he read an ad for a job on a chicken ranch just out of Denver. He got the job, such as it was. The salary was twenty-nine dollars a month plus a quart of milk and three eggs a day and a little house. The farmer even crabbed about our getting too many eggs. We were there at Christmas time, and I wanted a tree. We couldn't afford it. I cried so hard Hollis bought me one anyway, a big one. It cost twenty-five cents.

One Sunday we met an old college friend who had two trucks he hauled freight with. He hired Hollis to keep books and do flunky work. Dick and Edna lived in a two-story, four-bedroom house. We moved in with them and paid rent from the thirty-five dollars a month salary we were getting.

I went to a teachers' agency in Denver, even though I knew a married woman probably wouldn't be hired. Surprisingly, there was an opening for a married couple in a remote area in southern Colorado near the New Mexico border. Jarosa was the name of the town. The farming community surrounding Jarosa was in the valley of a plateau in the Rockies, with an altitude of over 6,000 feet. Irrigated farms raised lettuce and produce. A train

113

passed by once a day. Seemed like it always went north, but it must have gone south too. Jarosa had a post office, a store, a garage, a Pentacostal church and a Seventh Day Adventist church. And the school, of course, which had two rooms divided by folding doors.

In my class, I had one red-headed white boy. The rest were Mexican and Japanese. I was invited to Japanese all-day celebrations where the favorite food seemed to be hard-boiled eggs, and where my pupils in lovely Japanese costumes, danced.

People were sociable. They had to be; they were so isolated. There was plenty to do. We shopped and went to movies in Alamosa, fifteen miles away, played a lot of bridge, shot prairie dogs, went coyote hunting and deer hunting during the season and went fishing in the mountains.

One summer vacation from teaching, we worked for a small lumber operation run by two brothers. We lived in a small mountain cabin with a creek running alongside.

Families relocated in the Jarosa area from the dust bowl of Oklahoma, Kansas and Nebraska, an area of the south that had lost its topsoil due to drought and high winds that blew the dust in fence-high piles like snowdrifts.

The county had paid us our seventy-five dollars a month by check, but in our third year, the county ran out of money and issued us instead of checks, warrants that no bank would cash. Private companies in Denver would cash them for a substantial discount. We had to find another school. Hollis found a midterm job in Gillette, Wyoming, but I finished the year out where I was. I opened up the folding doors and taught all grades, one to nine. The one ninth grader was a Japanese boy. We got along fine except for general science. When he reached the subject of machines in his text book, all I could do was give him assignments and A's. I didn't understand a thing about machines.

On the last day of school in 1938, I headed for Wyoming by taking a train to Alamosa and transferring at Alliance. The conductor came by my seat to look at my ticket. Then he looked at me and said, "You're on the wrong train. You're on the way back to where you came from." Two trains had come into the terminal at the same time, and I got on the wrong one. I cried all the way back. To make connections, I had to wait several hours, so I went shopping. I can still remember the dress I bought that day. It was a light blue shirtwaist dress of woven material with many brown buttons. Buying a new dress or hat always makes a woman feel better. By the time I arrived and found Hollis waiting, I felt okay. Actually, he wouldn't have been able to meet me if I'd been on the other train; he'd have been in school.

Hollis was still teaching in Gillette when Jan, our son, was born in 1939 and Ruth, whom I call Sandy, in 1941. When she was born, I didn't like the hometown doctors so went to one in Sheridan, fifteen miles away. We had no car so had to take the train which was what happened when Ruth arrived. We took the train on one day and she was born the next. Hollis was with me, and Mama took my place at home.

Our last year in Gillette, Hollis changed from teaching to managing a feed store. When the children were seven and four, we moved to Casper, Wyoming and a better job. That was in 1945. We bought a house a block from the children's school and lived there until the children were ten and seven.

The winter of 1949-50 was so cold the temperature at times didn't even register on the thermometer. I remember making a trip out once in minus fifty degrees. It started snowing at Thanksgiving. Snowdrifts were house-high. Some called it a "haydrop winter" because cattle couldn't move in the snow to feed, so hay shipped in by plane from Idaho and California had to be dropped to the farms. If the farmers were lucky, the hay would be near the barn. It's hard to believe how cold it was; you could *see* the cold.

That's when we decided to move to California. Hollis would only work at a job so long; then he'd wear out. We sold the house and headed west though we didn't know where we'd end up. It turned out to be Carlsbad. Hollis found work at Convair, an airplane factory, while I substitute taught at Oceanside and Carlsbad. Later I taught grade one full-time. We bought a house, finished raising the children and I taught for twenty years. During that time, in 1970 to be exact, our marriage broke up after many years of increasing incompatibility. I still don't like to think about it or talk about it, and I don't.

I loved teaching in Carlsbad. Activity in the teachers' organization, not a union, kept me busy after school. They asked me to be president, and I thought I needed something to give me more self-confidence in front of groups. I joined the Toastmistress Club; it really helped. Schools were changing with increased political involvement. Legislators began to tell us how to teach. Increasing paperwork took the joy out of teaching. I was almost glad when I got a Dear John letter telling me I was almost sixty-five and had to retire, as if I didn't already know it. Farewell parties highlighted my retirement. I cleaned out my desk, said goodbye to my students and colleagues and left teaching forever.

The time has come to do something different—something I had never done before. I got myself a real estate license and worked at that for four years and then retired from working for good. One of the different things I did during that period was to wear a wig. I've always had a problem with my hair because it's so fine. So I bought a wig, a handsome blond wig from Paris. It was surprisingly comfortable. I loved it. I even went to my favorite hair dresser, Johnny, who liked to fuss with it as if it were my own hair.

During that period, I met Wilmoth W. Watkins. His colleagues called him W.W., but I always called him Wilmoth. He was a real estate broker and had his own firm. He had served for twenty years in the Marine Corps and had retired as a captain. A former wife died of cancer. They had no children. Wilmoth was ten years younger than I, which made no difference whatsoever. We never imagined anything could happen to us like our wonderful relationship. We got married in 1975, sold our houses and bought a beautiful home on Portofino Drive in Oceanside. We did everything together. We even had two vacuum cleaners and two lawn mowers.

We hired a housesitter to care for the house and the dog and took some trips. Japan was our first goal. Wilmoth had been there during the war and thought I might enjoy it. I did, but I also thought the floating vegetable markets in Bangkok were colorful, the people of Hong kong were pushy and that Singapore was an unexpectedly beautifully laid out city.

In Europe, our favorite town was Lucerne. We loved it for its old-world quaintness. In Florence, we exhausted ourselves taking in the art galleries, as does everyone else, I suppose. I had taught about Rome but not that it was so dirty; that was a surprise. In Paris, it seemed people disliked Americans; it felt uncomfortable.

Then we visited Tahiti, New Zealand and Australia but mostly New Zealand. Every place we went there we would say, "I want to live here." I hadn't seen Washington yet. Later when I did, it reminded me of New Zealand.

After we got home from that trip, Wilmoth went to the doctor for a physical checkup. The doctor discovered a cancer. He had surgery twice and never really recovered. A year and a half later, on June 7, 1980, I lost my Wilmoth.

After his death, I tried to stay in the house we had planned to live in the rest of our lives, but the house kept getting bigger and bigger, and the lawn needed mowing oftener and oftener. My daughter, Ruth, had been transferred to Seattle by the National Labor Relations Board for which she worked. She and her husband bought a house on Mercer Island and at Christmas time, I came up to visit. After a few days I said, "I'm going to move to Washington. There's no reason in the world I can't live where I want to." I wanted to be in the northwest not only because of Ruth but because of the environment so similar to the New Zealand we had loved. I went home, saw son Jan through bypass surgery and recuperation, rented the house and came north.

On my eightieth birthday, Ruth gave me a party. Sybil, my oldest sister came up from Oakland, and Beth from Troutdale, Oregon. Ruth had invited her friend, Cathy, and husband. My birthday cake had eighty candles on it. It's amazing how much heat is generated by eighty little candles. With Cathy's help, I got them all blown out. Ruth had collected eighty garnets and strung them into a necklace for my gift. Someone read a poem and gave it to me. I've remembered it ever since.

Age is a quality of mind.
If you have left your dreams behind,
if hope is gone,
if you no longer look ahead,
if your ambition fires are dead,
then you're old.

But if to life you give your best,
and if for life you have a zest,
no matter how the moments fly,
no matter how the years roll by,
you are not old.

It happened friends of Ruth's had been living in a rental house on Yeomalt Point Drive on Bainbridge Island until they bought a home of their own. They found their new house and thought I should try the place on Yeomalt. I was intrigued by the view of Puget Sound, Seattle and the Cascades. It didn't take long to realize Bainbridge was where I wanted to stay. I needed my own home, so in April, 1987, I moved into my little gray house with the blue door. I intend to stay here as long as I live.

Bainbridge is just different from anywhere else I have lived. I've never been any place where people were so friendly, and I could make so many friends in such a short time. Having lived in California, I appreciate the lack of congestion on the island—no traffic tieups. And the leisurely, relaxed feeling that surrounds me is just right.

Life is very satisfying now. I realize how lucky I am. My health is perfect—no problems. How rare for an eighty-year-old. I even have trouble making myself go to the doctor for an annual physical.

The children are loving and attentive. Sybil, who has no children of her own, says I'm unusually close to mine. Son Jan, who remains in California, has two children. Gary will soon be a junior at the University of California. He married a girl with a two-year old daughter which makes me a step great-grandmother. His sister, Laura, worked her way up to manager of a shoe store in the two years since she left high school. Ruth, my own daughter, is still on Mercer Island and has twenty-year-old Philese in Bellevue Community College and Sharon still in high school.

I keep busy all the time. First I had to clean the new house to suit me; the yard also needed work. Then came the time to harvest the six fruit trees, can the fruit and make jelly. I do some maintenance on the house, like painting. Friends and relatives from California want to see how I'm living now, so I've had one batch of company after another. One of my neighbors commented this summer, "Every time I look at your driveway, I see a different car." Ruth visits almost every weekend, and I keep in touch with Jan by telephone.

I serve lunches at the Senior Center twice a week and play bridge there on Tuesdays and any other time someone asks me. I want to keep active. I think it keeps me feeling young.

I've never really thought about age and hope I don't worry about it when I become old. I feel I still have promises to keep. I want to see the year 2,000 come in and travel many more miles before I sleep. I'm not old. ❦

Bertha Jones

BERTHA STEVENS JONES, the oldest of our ten storytellers, is a pretty, feminine-looking lady who often wears frilly and lacy blouses. She is a woman of several talents—music, drama and art, with an interest emphasis on art. Until recently, she had managed the Bridge Club for several years. For two years, she taught an art class at the Center.

Bertha Jones

"When the horse wanted a drink, he took one prong of the crossbar handle of the hydrant in his mouth and turned it on. The trouble was he couldn't turn it off."

One of my goals in life has been to live to be ninety years old. Since I was born on June 5, 1898, and am now eighty-nine, it looks as if I might make it.

I was born in Erie, Colorado, a small town in the southern part of the state, not quite at the foot of the Rockies. Erie was named after another coal town in Pennsylvania. In our area were several deposits of bituminous coal and many productive farms. Later, oil was discovered. Of the population of about 1,000, the miners were mostly first generation immigrants from Wales, England or France and the farmers had come from Germany, Scandinavia and Russia

Father, George Stevens, was a dark-haired, wiry man. He came from Gloucestershire, England, the twelfth of fourteen children. His parents had sailed for America, leaving only one son who stayed behind because he loved his home and had no desire to emigrate. While aboard ship, Father's sister, Alice, age eighteen, died and was buried at sea. His father, a Presbyterian minister and miner, decided to head for the coal fields in Illinois. Later, he followed a brother to Erie, Colorado.

Dad liked to run, and entered many races. One time a competitor who came to town to race told Dad if he won, he would be knifed. He ran anyway and won, but nothing happened. He stopped running for years, but when he was sixty, he ran a race barefoot at a picnic and still won.

When I was very young, Dad worked at the Old Lister Coal Mine about two miles out of town. There was no public or any other kind of transportation, so he walked to and from work. I remember him coming home at night covered with black coal dust and carrying his dinner bucket. People who didn't understand, sometimes called the men "dirty old miners." Our comeback was, "They're the cleanest men in town because they take a bath every day." Baths were hard to come by in those days because the water had to be carried in and then heated. He earned thirteen to fifteen dollars a month and worked twelve or thirteen hours a day. A few days after payday, there wasn't money to buy even a two-cent stamp. They had no machinery, so he worked with pick and shovel. Coal had to be moved to the mouth of the shaft by wooden carts drawn by mules. It was abusive work for the mules. They were kept down in the mine all winter. In the summer, they were put out to pasture. At the same time, the men had to find work elsewhere because there was no demand for coal in the summer.

Mother came from Ohio, and her name was Ella Walter. She was taller than Dad—tall and slender. Her eyes were blue, and she rolled her blond hair up in back. She graduated from Erie High School in 1893, and after graduation, became a housemaid until she met and married Dad in 1897. Besides taking care of us and the house, she was active in the Rebecca Lodge, as was I when I grew older. It was a secret sister organization, religious in nature, but not sectarian. It did a great many things for charity.

I was born at home and for seventeen years was an only child. We lived in a small house in town that had been remodeled from a chicken coop. At least, that was the family story. Since there was no pavement even in town, the house was on a dirt road. There was a shed outside. I remember once I was put in that shed for punishment, and I saw a small mouse peering out at me from its hole. I screamed and cried until Mother came to get me.

Another time I was scared when I saw a red devil walking down the street. Mother explained he was just dressed like a devil to advertise Red Devil Stove Cleaner, and he really wasn't anyone to fear.

We had a pet dog named Nig. He died, and we had a real funeral with prayers and sermon and all. Mother and Dad were there and an uncle, who was on his way to Illinois from the Philippines. He brought his own dog with him, and it wouldn't eat anything but bananas. Its presence at our house made the loss of Nig easier to bear. When Uncle left, he took his dog with him.

When I was six, we moved to a new house across from an elementary school. I really liked being close to school. I liked everything about the school, too, but especially language and art. We almost never had discipline problems, although once in a while a student, usually a boy, would have to stand in the corner. Kids were different in those days. You either behaved, or you didn't get to go to school.

After school, we studied or played Run Sheep Run and other games. Or we would go up a hill to a ditch where we could catch beetles we called "wishing bugs." We would make our wishes and then put the bugs back in the ditch. I never told anyone about my wish; it was always the same. I wanted Mother to have a baby. All the other kids had brothers and sisters, and I didn't.

It seemed to me we had a very happy home. I

125

helped Mother with the housework, especially later when she worked at the store Dad had bought when he left mining. Then I did the cooking sometimes. I took piano lessons from the time I was eight until I was fifteen and did a lot of accompanying for programs at school and church, but music was never my first love. Art was, especially watercoloring.

On Sundays, Mother took me to the Methodist Sunday school, and after that, I sang in the choir in church. I always had a part in the Christmas programs.

In fact. I became quite a performer. Opera companies came to town and frequently would need a local child to complete their casts. Somehow, I got drawn into that and learned how to sing and act on stage. I don't remember being scared at all. I loved it. Later, I felt more adult when I took part in high school plays.

When I was in the eighth grade, Dad went back to the old trade of cigar-making by hand he had learned in Illinois when he was eighteen. He took a job in Boulder about fourteen miles away. We rented the house in Erie. In Boulder, our new landlord's son, Charles, was my age. He had a friend, James, who was a black boy. Erie didn't have any black people, so I had never seen one before. Both boys were in my class in school and we would go home after classes and play different games. I adored them both.

We only lived there a year. Then we moved back to Erie where Dad ran the small grocery store. A house was attached to the store, and there was a window between, so we could always see what was going on. One time, Dad had just brought a new load of fruit from the depot. An old woman came into the store, walked toward the back and filled her blouse with newly-bought apples and oranges. I saw her and went out to the store and said, "That's nice fruit you picked out." I thought I was paying her a compliment, but she quickly dropped the fruit and ran out of the store and didn't come back for a long time.

One snowy night, the bakery next door began to burn. The distance between the two buildings was only two feet. Volunteer firemen got on top of the roof and packed snow between the buildings. The bakery was destroyed, but our building was saved. However, during the fracas, vandals took from our store hundred-pound sacks of flour and sugar and whatever else they could get ahold of.

We had a horse that was named after Fitzsimmons, the prizefighter. He used to bring food from the depot to the store. Our little dog liked to ride on the back of Fitzsimmons; I still have a photograph of them. When the horse wanted a drink, he took one prong of the crossbar handle of the hydrant in his mouth and turned it on. The trouble was he couldn't turn it off.

For a change once in a while, Mother and I would go to Boulder Canyon where Grandfather Walter owned a gold mine. My three young aunts and I had wonderful times gathering wildflowers, huckleberries and strawberries on the mountainside. I still have a little ring made from gold Grandfather dug.

One day, Father was mowing the lawn when I came out into the yard having just bathed and readied myself to go someplace. He asked me to hose the lawn, which I refused to do because I was all dressed up. He didn't like that, so he turned the hose on me, much to my humiliation.

Another time, Mother left town as a delegate to

some convention, so Dad and I batched it. I caught a cold. Dad said, "I know what I must do. I'll make you some candy." He made candy all right—with cayenne pepper in it. I surely won't forget that candy, but it did the trick.

The town had a smallpox epidemic. Mother had only one pock but was quarantined. Dad stayed at the hotel, but I was with Mother. I never did get the disease. We used to look out the window and laugh at the neighbors as they carefully walked down the middle of the road past our house for fear of contamination. A pest house down by the creek was set up for the most serious cases.

As an only child, I had every imaginable toy. My friend, Ella, lived across the street, and because there were six kids in her family, she didn't have much. But she did have a hayloft. So I took my equipment, furniture and all, over to the hayloft to share with Ella. One day her older brother came home and threw everything of mine out of the loft. I think he was jealous because he had to work and Ella didn't. Actually, Ella *was* working, taking care of her little brother—sort of. Every once in a while, she would call his name, and as long as he answered, "Here I are in the alleyway," she felt free to play with me. Ella, who lives in Oregon, is one of the few old friends I still see.

There were also the times when I kicked one of my new shoes at a boy playmate, and it landed in the creek; when Dad went to Denver in a snowstorm and came back covered with lice; and when my folks gave me a grand piano for Christmas.

When I was seventeen, Mother became pregnant. At last we were going to have a baby. We moved back to our original home which had been rented, so we would have more room. Dad sold the grocery store and bought a much larger general store, which he managed until retirement. When the baby boy arrived, he was named Lawrence. I took care of him so willingly and so much while Mother worked at the store that he actually thought I was his mother.

Just before he was born, we had a scary experience. During a lightning storm, Mother walked over to the sink for a drink. A ball of fire as big as a hand plopped into the sink from the faucet. It was round and fiery red. After a moment it went on down the drain. We had never seen anything like it.

I liked everything about high school, especially art. I learned to be comfortable in many media. When I graduated, I was one point away from being valedictorian. There were only two of us in the class. Nevertheless, graduation exercises were in the opera house.

After high school I went to college in Greeley to study art. I played basketball and started dating. We went to parties, on buggy rides and saw some of the first motion pictures. I would pack my pockets and the lining of my coat with goodies from the store and share them with my friends.

One day we had an experience on campus some people would have trouble believing. It was noontime. The campus was filled with students. We all saw the U.F.O. hovering above the trees. It was about the size of a plane, but it was long and round and just stayed in place. It stayed there until just before time to return to classes. No one had any lunch that day.

Another time I saw a U.F.O. I was with a teaching friend. We went to an outdoor movie in her car. I saw this object that didn't move in the sky. I told Pauline, and we watched the U.F.O. instead of the movie. As the movie was over, it left.

I met Raymond Jones and he wanted to date me, and I was very pleased. He was tall, and I thought him handsome. He had moved to town from Iowa. We went together for about a year, and then on September 3, 1917, we got married. It was a very small wedding. We took off for Denver with a couple of friends and my parents. There was no honeymoon.

Ray's father had bought a large farm. We moved into its lovely big house with Mr. Jones and his grown family. World War I was under way and the government needed farm products. We fed and made ready for market a herd of cattle and also harvested huge crops of sugarbeets.

After the war, the family gave up farming and moved back to Erie, but we stayed on for three years while Ray walked three miles to and from a job in a coal mine. I was alone all day long, and during that time, I had a premature baby boy who only lived nine days. We were devastated. We wanted that baby so much.

A little house near the mine was our next home. In 1919, Elinor was born. For over thirty years after that, our lives were full raising our five remaining children. The first two were born a year apart. The doctor said it would be dangerous for me to have any more children. After nine years, we decided we'd take the risk and go ahead and have a child anyway. We proceeded to have three.

Elinor and Sally, the first and last, were girls. Sally and Don were premature and needed tender, loving care. We didn't think Don would ever walk. He was still sitting on the ground paddling himself along at nineteen months; one day he grabbed the handles of Elinor's buggy, pulled himself up, and away he went. He hasn't stopped yet. Three are exceptionally musical. Wendal was head of the music department at the University of Arizona. Elinor is still singing in the Episcopal choir and in Gay Nineties Revues for the Senior Center. Sally became a music specialist and teaches piano on Bainbridge. All were graduated from Erie High School. Although each was involved in World War II in his own way, Kenneth was the only one sent overseas. He was in the Air Force for four years, and at one point, his plane carried President Roosevelt to Europe.

Mother and Father were both killed accidentally. Mother had gone blind and was in a rest home in Colorado. She was being raised off her bed when the pulley broke, and she hit her head on the iron bed. Just before she died, Dad was driving in a snowstorm to see her and slid off the road into a ditch. He was able to get out of the car and onto the road, but another car came along and hit him.

During World War II, I accumulated enough credits at Greenley College and at the University of Colorado at Boulder to get a teacher's certificate and a Master's Degree. I began teaching and continued until retirement in 1963.

Ray had a heart attack. He lived for several years. Then one day when I started out to go to the beauty parlor where he usually drove me, he said, "Would you care if I didn't go with you today?" "Of course not," I said. When I got back, he asked, "Would you mind if I lie down for a while?" Within minutes, I heard a gurgling sound. I thought it was the sink, but I went into the bedroom to check. He had passed on. I've always been grateful he went peacefully and didn't suffer. It was February 1, 1964 when my beloved husband, age sixty-nine, entered eternal life.

Sally thought I should come to Bainbridge, so I did. I did a lot of painting and walked five miles a day when I first moved here. I applied to teach in the Bainbridge schools and was asked to teach full time, but I chose to substitute. Each spring I got a letter from school asking me to teach the following year. It gave me a good feeling, since I was in my seventies. Our first bridge club started with one table twenty years ago and is still going, now at the Senior Center. Until recently, I managed it. One year, during the Spokane World's Fair, I took care of two grandchildren while their musician parents played ninety-eight gigs with the symphony at the Fair. Last summer, my younger brother, now seventy-three, came to visit. It is still a treat to be together.

The last two years I have entered the two-month long senior art show, "Dreams of Retirement," at Arts and Crafts. Recently, I had a successful eye implant and now have 20/20 vision once more.

I have promised my family for many years I would write a short, informative account of my family history so they can know better where they come from and how they got where they are. It has been a pleasure finally to get the story recorded, and I appreciate the help I've gotten.

Chesley
A.
Smith

CHESLEY ALFRED (C.A.) SMITH is a six-foot, one-inch man with a thatch of white hair, a ruddy Norwegian complexion and a mustache.

He was appointed to the original board of the Bainbridge Island Senior Community Center as an alternate delegate from the Dona Center, an already existing senior group. He became BISCC's first full term treasurer and has served on the nominating committee. He was an original member of the Omega Senior Chorus, and his bass voice became an integral part of the Drama Group revues.

He drops in at the Center frequently, although he is no longer active.

♥ Chesley A. Smith ♥

"One thing I learned from raising daughters was how to get along with women. I had to; it was a matter of survival."

I was born the day after Christmas in 1905 in Ferndale, California near Eureka. The story goes that I was actually born on Christmas, but so late it was decided December 26th would be a better birthday so it could be separate from Christmas Day. Dad was running a small cannery on the Eel River for Talent-Grant Packing company of Astoria, Oregon. The project was an experiment which was abandoned a year later, and we moved back to Astoria where I grew up.

We lived in a small four room house on Kensington Avenue which was adequate for the time. Around the corner lived my earliest friend, Harold Haddan. Before we could even say mama and papa, we were calling each other Aba and Awa. I was Aba. Our mothers were friends so Awa and I spent a great deal of time together. Since I was three months older, I started school first. Hal says that to this day, he remembers how it felt to look out the window and watch me deserting him.

When we were seven or eight, we played with Ruth and Esther Snow. One day we all went down to a swamp in a deep gully (forbidden to us, but we went anyway). We liked to catch frogs there. Esther fell in the water, and as she was going under, I grabbed her hair as I held on to a bough on the bank. I imagined I saved her life, but I had heard somewhere that if you saved a life, it belonged to you, and I didn't really want to be saddled with any

135

girl at that time.

I wasn't happy with school. It seemed the old maid teachers were pretty crotchety and didn't really like the kids. In high school I liked some of the teachers, but mainly I liked football. In that I excelled.

What I really enjoyed was fishing—even on school days. On my bike I pedalled out Young's River Road to fish in the river for cutthroat trout. I always came home with fish even though I hated cleaning them.

I enjoyed the woods and was a pretty good woodsman. I never went anyplace I couldn't get back from; I never got lost. I liked being alone. It was quiet, although when I was still enough myself, I could hear all kinds of activities—squirrels, chipmunks, wood mice, fox, the wind in the trees and the sound of the stream.

World War I started when I was nine. Boys were asked to gather in gunnysacks foxglove leaves for making digitalis for the army. Silent movies were full of horror stories about the Huns and their atrocities like bayoneting babies, stories designed to stir up hatred of the enemy. Women thought our boys would go over and win the war in short order, but when the casualty lists appeared, including names of friends and relatives, they became more sober about their flagwaving, knitting and winding bandages. The war was no longer a lark.

Among my happiest childhood memories were visits to my grandparent's farm in Washington. I would take the river boat across the Columbia to Megler (There's a bridge there now) and get on the little narrow gauge railway called the Clamshell Special that carried Astorians and others to their Long Beach summer homes. At Wallacut Junction, I would get off and walk through the flatlands to some wooded hills, carrying my bag. It was dark and scary. I would imagine panthers and black bears. Once I actually saw a panther crouched on a fallen tree overhead, but he paid no attention to me. It was an exciting seven and a half miles to the farm.

The farm was out on a peninsula overlooking a saltwater marsh on Showalter Bay. The grazing was excellent, but after a day of it, the cattle would run up the hill for fresh water to get some of the salt out of their systems.

I fished and hunted. Hunting I didn't like, though I was able to prove to my grandfather that I could shoot by bringing a bluejay down from the top of a hemlock tree. I never told him it was an accident.

When haying season came, I was needed to drive the haywagon drawn by four oversized horses. The hay was down on the flatland, and we would fill the wagon, take it up to the barn and lift it to the second story with a hay fork powered by horses.

We had enormous vegetables because the garden was located where a chicken house had been. Everything was put up for the winter. Salmon and geese were packed in salt brine. Vegetables and fruits were canned by water bath. Only such staples as salt, sugar, flour and beans were needed during the winter.

Grandma was about half my size, even then, the cutest little lady you ever saw, and smart as a whip. Eventually she worked herself to death—just died in her sleep of exhaustion it seemed. I remember her telling me, "You should never say you don't like something given you to eat. You should say, 'Grandma, I like this so well, I want to save it for tomorrow'." I am a replica of Grandpa, I am told, except that he was dark complexioned. He had a gravel-ly wavery voice and had a joke for every occasion.

Just before school was out, when I was twelve, my Dad asked, "How would you like to come work on the seining ground this summer?" I could hardly believe my good luck. They cooked up a job which didn't amount to much, but made me feel important. In the bow of the seining skiff, they made a rope loop I could sit in. When the bow would begin to swing, I would dig my feet in the sand to stop the motion. That was my job. There were several seining skiffs with nets. A launch would pull each skiff out into the water, anchor one end of the net, and spread the rest of it around in a semicircle back to the shore where it was attached to the beach by a hauling line. As the outgoing tide pulled at the nets, they would fill with fish. Then the nets would be pulled in by a team of horses. These horses were trained for this kind of work—to side-step, one foot over the other, so they could move ashore and down the beach at the same time. I think some of those horses wore lots smarter than the kids who were driving them. There was a skiff crew, beach crew, skinners who drove the horses, and launchmen— about thirty men altogether. Dad ran the operation. Later, when I was nineteen or twenty I ran a seining ground of my own.

Seining is now outlawed and is a colorful part of the past.

Because of the seining, I got close to my father and always admired him. Dad was a big handsome man who resembled President Roosevelt in appearance. He had a sense of humor and often got his ideas across in the form of silly verses. He liked me too.

Not so, Mother. I just wasn't what she thought a man would be. He should be a banker or a store owner in town, wear a white collar, have summer, not winter, vacations and be genteel. The differences between her ideas and Dad's led to a divorce when I was fifteen, an unusual event in those days. A year later they remarried and when I was seventeen I had a little brother, Bob, whom I never did know well.

At eighteen I started college at the University of Oregon at Eugene, still working with Dad in the summers. In my sophomore year, I transferred to Oregon State at Corvallis in order to get the courses I wanted in Business Administration. I liked Oregon State better because the kids were more down to earth it seemed to me. I lived at the Alpha Tau Omega house where I was popular in the spring because of my possible influence in helping my classmates get summer jobs. I didn't do too well in school. I had too much money. It took my time spending it.

At the end of my third college year, in 1929, I ran out of money because of the Depression and had to quit school. There were no jobs for either Dad or me. We tried making sandwich spreads of sturgeon and kippered fish, but no one had money to buy. There was too much competition, and we didn't know how to market, anyway. The only item which succeeded for a while was kippered steelhead trout and our only customers were in the Jewish community. When they knew my truck was coming to deliver the fish, they would stand in the street wringing their hands and drooling at the mouth. They would grab the fish and start eating as soon as they got ahold of it. We couldn't get enough steelhead to fill the demand. It was even koshered by the Rabbi.

Even though we got a dollar a pound for this

item, it wasn't enough to support us, so Dad found me a job as tank truck salesman for the Union Oil Company at $100 a month. I was one of the few lucky kids who had work. They sent me to Kelso, Washington.

One of my runs was up to Spirit Lake. There I met Harry Truman who was later killed when Mt. St. Helens blew. He was quite a character. He tamed deer, raccoon and all kinds of animals. He swore almost every other word. But he was interesting.

From Kelso, I was transferred to Winlock, so-called egg capital of Washington. I liked the area and the people. I lived in Mrs. Miller's boarding house with ten schoolteachers. One of them I kind of liked. Her name was Phoebe. "Here's one I think I could live with," I thought. So I proposed to her one night while we were parked by the railroad track waiting for the Royal Scot, a famous train shipped over from Scotland, to go by. I'd been to a stag party where I'd had some drinks, but I asked her, anyway, to marry me.

"Don't ask me now. Ask me tomorrow," she said. So I did, and we were engaged. We didn't tell anyone, because teachers were not supposed to be tied up in any way at that time. But of course people were talking about us because we were together a lot. So we decided to get married before the end of the term. Without confiding in anyone except a friend of Phoebe's, Dolores Tinkcom, we drove to Shelton, Washington on a sunny Saturday morning, a St. Patrick's Day, and got married at the court-house. I was so nervous I said "I do" several times, but we got through it.

Soon after, we did tell our parents who greeted the news with varying degrees of enthusiasm. When school was out in June, Phoebe came to live with me in Centralia where I was then stationed. I had no money except what I was earning. Phoebe's salary was $68 a month as a teacher, and she had her summer pay of $204 which we used to pay bills, so we started our married life free and clear financially—but just barely.

Two years and a baby girl later I lost the job, and in 1937, we decided to move to Seattle where Phoebe's parents lived. I sold my banjo for $6, arranged for temporary storage of the Weber piano Phoebe had enjoyed since she was sixteen, packed our meager possessions in "Lousy Fenders," our ancient four-cylinder Dodge roadster with the snap-on side curtains, and barely made it to Seattle.

I tramped around the town in shoes filled with cardboard to cover the holes, while Phoebe tried to make a home in a housekeeping room containing a two-burner hotplate and twin beds. Sylvia, the baby, slept in a dresser drawer.

In two weeks I found a job at Wold's Super Service where I tried to collect money from the county assessor and his staff who had been buying gas, oil and tires on credit—an arrangement agreed to by Mr. Wold, because the assessor was a drinking partner of his.

"I don't care how you do it. Just get the money any way you can," said Mr. Wold. Since ordinary collection methods had failed up to now, the only way I could figure out to do it was to sue the county and the assessors; so I filed the suits. When Mr. Wold learned what I had done, he nearly collapsed because both he and the assessor had been billing the county for goods it had not received, and he was afraid the suits might reveal this activity. So I was forced to withdraw the suits, and I was out of a job again.

141

After that, life was a series of short-term jobs—anything I could find to keep the family alive. I tried to sell insurance to people who wanted it, but couldn't afford it; they offered me geese, chickens, eggs—whatever they did have, as down payment. I tried selling down quilts house to house; again people wanted them but couldn't afford them. I tried selling nuts, bolts and screw products for a company whose woman manager refused to pay the salaries agreed upon until she had to. I was becoming pretty discouraged.

While I was selling quilts, I had met Eddie Bauer. When World War II started, he asked me to manage a factory manufacturing down jackets and sleeping bags for the troops. Because of this, I learned later, I was not drafted for military service, or maybe it was because I had reached the age limit of thirty-eight. Four hundred women in three shifts worked to produce those bags and jackets—all kinds of women, wealthy ones, prostitutes, young and old. Just keeping the peace was a challenge.

When the war was over, so was the job. Steve Antoncich, one of my former associates with Eddie Bauer, suggested starting a business making fishing lures. This worked well until Steve brought a sister up from California to invest and work in the business, and this did not work.

A friend recommended me to Harold Barde to sell steel in eastern Washington. There was a shortage of steel at the time, so it was more a matter of taking orders than a hard sell. Also my previous selling experience came in handy. I did well and felt good about it. I had finally found something I really liked. Mr. Barde was appreciative; I liked travelling; many of my customers became friends. During the summer months, I would camp out instead of using a motel room. I would buy steaks, cook them over an open fire and serve them to selected customers. It was more fun and far less expensive than restaurants. I stayed in the steel business until I retired at sixty-four.

In October of that year, a heart condition caused me to black out on the freeway. I seesawed down an offramp and came to a stop at the bottom. Surprisingly, although the rented car was a total wreck, I only needed eight stitches in my forehead. I had survived the experience, but it seemed wiser to reduce stress as much as possible. One way to do this was to stop working. Fortunately I was close enough to retirement age for it to be financially possible, so I gave notice and ended my work life.

There have been times when I wished I could have stayed with seining or finished my education for a career. As it was, work to me was not an end in itself; it was a means to an end. The end was living. When my work life was over, I was emotionally free to enjoy my retirement years with hardly a backward glance.

The other important aspect of my life was my family. Being a family man was something I had never considered seriously. The present was always too full to look ahead. Marriage just happened, and so did the first child. Every step of the way came as a surprise up until then.

We floundered through the first two years of our marriage, establishing our roles, learning to live together, worrying about money.

Then we had a child. Because she was a new experience, I was especially impressed by Sylvia Chesley. She was small, but she was a real person and so dependent that my feeling of responsibility grew a hundredfold—and my awareness of how important a tiny person can be.

Three years and two months later, Susan Emily was born. We hadn't really planned for her either, but there she was. Why she was so accident prone when she was little, I don't know, but she kept hitting her head in the same place so often I was sure she would have a permanent lump.

When the girls were about six and nine, Phoebe had the idea of family meetings to discuss shared problems. I was elected president, and no sooner had I called the first meeting to order than Sylvia stood to say, "Mr. President, I move this family have a baby." A year later, we did have another baby girl and named her Jennifer Jeanne. (Her grandmother thought the name sounded too much like Walla Walla.) When Susan saw the baby for the first time, she said, "It's too bad she's a girl. Now there's no one to carry on the family name."

I enjoyed the girls when they were children. They would run to greet me when I came home at night. They needed me to repair their toys. I became a doctor, a secret dream of mine, when they were hurt. And they were full of surprises.

When Jennifer was six months old, we went on our first camping trip, using quilts and blankets since we had no equipment, and sleeping on the hard ground. Little by little we accumulated sleeping bags and air mattresses, a stove, lantern and tent until we could camp in comparative comfort and safety. With Glen and Marian Fairbanks, who also had three daughters, we would pile into my panel delivery truck and sing all the way to the ocean or park.

There had been little music in my early life, and I had missed it without knowing. Phoebe could both sing and play the piano. She composed, directed choruses, took lessons and taught piano. Eventually she taught music and grade six at View Ridge Elementary School. The girls were introduced to music at an early age. I never minded listening to any of them practice. It was sort of fulfilling. I also discovered I liked the sound of my own voice, as did my family.

So much of my time was spent working and travelling that I couldn't be home very much. Phoebe seemed to me to be in possession of the girls and at times I was resentful and felt like an outsider. We didn't always agree on discipline, but I couldn't do much about it from eastern Washington, which was frustrating.

When they became teenagers, I felt even worse. It seemed like they weren't the same people; they had grown horns. Watching them get into cars with young punks whose driving I hadn't approved was painful. Going to the door to face slender young men I had to look up to was humiliating. Not knowing what they were doing or where they were exactly, as we had when they were younger, was frightening.

However, we got through it. They all graduated from high school; two went on to college; they all married at nineteen and were on their own. But that's another story.

One thing I did learn from raising daughters was how to get along with women. I had to; it was a matter of survival. I often wonder how life would have been different if we had had a son.

The most exciting part of our lives was our fifteen travel years. We always travelled on our own and always on a shoestring, but we did travel. We sailed a thirty-eight foot ketch, the *Pampero*, to Acapulco, Mexico. We travelled the length of the Baja Peninsula in a green G.M. truck equipped with three bunks with storage underneath, before there was a road. A Yugoslav freighter, the *Tuhobic*, took us to Italy and around the boot to Adriatic ports. We flew over the Pole to England. Twice we visited the Hawaiian Islands. Our forty-foot cruiser, the *Phoebe M.*, sailed us through the Inside Passage to Glacier Bay and Sitka, Alaska. We bought a twenty-six-foot Silver Streak trailer and journeyed across Canada, around the United States and into Mexico.

During five winters we lived in a Shangri La of a trailer park called San Jose del Tajo about four miles south of Guadalajara, Mexico. Then, when I could no longer tolerate the 5,000-foot altitude because of high blood pressure, we wintered for five more years in another trailer park, Golden Village, in Hemet, California near Palm Springs.

Some highlights of those trips:

There was the time the *Pampero* exploded in Acapulco Harbor with five people aboard in forty feet of water 200 feet off the Yacht Club dock. Although we were hospitalized, we all managed to survive. A three week stay in a small upstairs clinic in downtown Acapulco was an adventure in itself. Most memorable were the nurses who called me El Toro because of my strong though painful recovery, and who cried when they had to spray my burns.

We found other Americans who were in trouble. One was a young mountain climber headed for Peru, who twisted his leg running around a swimming pool. An old man was turned over and over in the surf in front of El Presidente Hotel and broke his back. A wealthy widow from California aboard a luxurious cruiser threatened her husband with a gun and was asked to anchor out—way out. A lawyer from Chicago had just lost his second wife to cancer, and was on a protracted alcoholic binge. There were many others and their plights made us

146

feel less isolated.

I dropped a sealed bottle containing a letter and two cigarettes to Phoebe's Seattle sister, Jeanne, into the waters of the Straits of Messina between Italy and Sicily. Before we reached home, Jeanne had read the letter.

We recall the mistral storm on the Mediterranean, which blew across Spain from the Bay of Biscay. There was no way to keep up with the luggage as it slithered around the stateroom. Almost everyone aboard was seasick, except us.

In Alaska, we navigated the Wrangell Narrows, a narrow defile about twenty miles long between towering mountains. The channel meanders through the area, twisting and turning, and sometimes switching back on itself. If it were not well buoyed and lighted, it would be impossible to navigate. The buoys are so close together that it is necessary to keep track of them by number. It was a hair-raising and exhausting experience.

As we cruised through icebergs just out of Glacier Bay, we remembered that what we were seeing was only a part of what was there and wondered what might happen to the part of the boat under the water.

On Baja, our fourteen-year old granddaughter, Heidi, was our "trusty Indian guide", sitting in a tire on top of the cab of the truck, finding the best routes and ruts to follow. After two weeks of desert, where even an isolated ranch or oasis is called a town, and the 100 or more degree heat, we arrived at La Paz, swollen with sunburn and exhausted, ready for a Margarita and a shower.

We were surprised at the small size of the White House and Lexington Bridge; having heard about them all our lives, we expected them to be larger.

147

In England, again we saw places only read about before—the Tower of London, the Roman ruins at Bath, Stonehenge, York and its Cathedral.

On the 125-mile-an-hour train from London to Edinburgh, we talked to a young Australian rancher from the outback and a Japanese girl studying midwifery. We all spoke English, but what different sounds!

In the Lake country in England, we got off the train by mistake in a downpour and found a seventeenth certury bed and breakfast house with uneven floors, a lumpy bed, a toilet with a square seat of varnished wood, and excellent food.

These are only a few of the many memories we have of our travel years.

We had been living aboard the *Phoebe M.*, our forty-foot blue and white fiber-glass cruiser for eight years, tied up on Pier F at Shilshole Bay Marina. We enjoyed the life and our adventurous neighbors. We watched the comings and goings of yachts of all sizes, and often took off for a cruise ourselves at a whim.

One of our favorite sailing destinations was Bainbridge Island. We liked the small-town shopping, the clubhouse which expanded our living space, and for the grandchildren when they were aboard, the tire swing that flew out over the water.

In 1975, we moved to Bainbridge Island at the request of Seattle's Queen City Yacht Club to keep an eye on its outstation near Winslow's city park. There had been some vandalism at the clubhouse, and since we were retired and living aboard our boat, we could spend the summer on the island.

Within a month, we had decided to make Bainbridge our home and bought a mobile home, expecting that in time, we would build a log cabin in the woods.

We never did go back to the Marina. Two years later we sold the boat and became full time Bainbridge Islanders. And it is doubtful that we will ever build the cabin. We are satisfied where we are.

As of 1987, we have lived on the island for twelve years. I don't know which I like better, the people or the rural atmosphere.

The first day on the island we needed to go to the bank and were amazed at how friendly everyone was. It was as if they already knew us. Children spoke to us on the street as they whizzed by on their skateboards. Even the young people smiled. As we explored the town, we had a feeling of having been there a long time.

I enjoy going from one place to another through trees instead of closely packed buildings and telephone wires. And it's good to know that wherever I want to go, it's not a very long drive.

One thing we did four years ago was to encourage granddaughter Heidi who was having a hard time in Spokane adjusting to a broken marriage and the need to raise and support two children, to move to Bainbridge. The change has worked well for her, and we are pleased to be able to watch two great grandchildren grow up.

My health has deteriorated since moving here, a troublesome complex of high blood pressure, heart failure and resulting circulatory problems, and medication. In the last incident a year ago, I almost lost a leg to gangrene, but didn't due to an alert doctor. I don't know why, probably medication, but I went into a deep depression and wanted no more of life. Eventually, the depression lifted, the foot healed, and I face life again. In fact, I have appreciated life more this last year than ever before, in spite of limited activity.

I learn a great deal about what's happening on the Island from Phoebe. She has managed to use her boundless energy to work for Bainbridge Performing Arts, Helpline, the *Bainbridge Review*, to study writing and to help get a new senior center organized. I must say, though, that when I was ill, she dropped everything else and became a fine nurse. She said she didn't know how, but she did it.

Now I spend my time reading Louis L'Amour, Robin Cook and the *National Geographic*. I watch Phoebe come and go and discuss her activities. I watch television, especially news and football. I drop in at the Senior Center often and enter into programs like bridge and Gay 90's Revue. I manage to keep track of three daughters, three grand-daughters, three grandsons (one was killed in a car accident in March—Brett, Susan's older son), and three great grandchildren.

I've lived through a period of time that produced radio, television, automobiles, electric lights, airplanes, the atomic bomb and computers. I've survived two world wars and several others, the Great Depression, several earthquakes, a boat explosion and three major operations.

There have been good times and bad times, but mostly good. I think I've been a lucky man.

*Phoebe
Smith*

PHOEBE COOK SMITH, with her optimistic outlook, willingness to take on new challenges and boundless energy, shares her zest for life with her husband of fifty-four years, Chesley (C.A.).

Her talent as a pianist has graced many shows of Bainbridge Performing Arts and all of BISCC's productions. For four years, she was director of the Center's Omega Chorus.

Phoebe was instrumental in the founding of BISCC, working in practically every aspect of the Center operation with the same thoughtful attention to detail that is evident in the rest of her life.

A few years ago, she began to write and did a weekly column, "Senior Newsmakers," for the *Bainbridge Review*. She is a member of the Wednesday Writers and has used this support to develop stories and poems, several of which have been published. Many hours have been devoted to her newest writing project, *80 Candles*, generously donated to BISCC.

Joanne Wills
BISCC Director

❦ Phoebe Smith ❦

"Both sisters were attention getters. My system was to be a good little girl and play the piano."

In 1983, when I became a founding mother of Bainbridge Island Senior Community Center and went through the process of helping to give it life, some new experiences came my way. As my contacts with the Bainbridge community expanded, I learned to work comfortably with City Hall. I became part of the legal process of incorporation. I had to deal with strong differences of opinion. Fundraising became a challenge. And I had a hand in converting a house into an activity center.

A satisfying result for me of all this was an enhanced feeling of self-confidence, an awareness that almost anything I really wanted to do, whether I'd done it before or not, was worth a try, and I could probably do it.

I certainly had not always felt that way. As a child, I was painfully shy, a more acceptable description of insecurity and fear. When I say painful, that's what I mean. In grade school, it was hard to respond to the teacher's questions even if I knew the answers. As soon as I learned I had to stand up and speak with all those kids looking at me, I would begin to blush. The blush would start at my feet and make its way up to my face. By the time my face became red, I was hot all over. I also blushed when bookworm Edward, of the horn-rimmed glasses, described the Amazon women of Brazil who cut off a breast so they could handle their bows better. And when Isabelle stood up to recite and was so embar-

rassed she created a puddle on the floor beneath her,
I blushed again.

I remember still being afraid of teachers and
people in authority when I was in high school. Also,
fear made my pedal knee shake when I played piano
in performance. I learned to choose pieces that needed
no pedal like "Golliwog's Cakewalk" and "Perpetual
Motion." I envied other girls who could walk down
the hall at school arm in arm, chatting and
laughing. Then there was Gladys. Gladys lived next
door. She was small and cute and wore her hair in
the new short bob. Boys liked Gladys. Daily they
drove up to her place and honked, and she would run
out and jump in the rumble seat or next to the
driver, and off they'd go. I would watch, feeling
neglected and jealous. When she and her family
moved away, I was glad. One day I went to the butcher's to buy meat, and he asked me if I knew where
the family of Gladys moved. No, I didn't. Well,
could I find out because they had left without paying their bill. I found the address and gave it to the
butcher who gave me, in return, a small cellophane-
covered cake with light brown chocolate icing. What
could I do with it? I couldn't take it home without
raising questions I didn't want to answer. So I walked
to a bridge overlooking some railroad tracks and
stood at the rail and ate the whole cake. I felt awful,
and it was years before I could look at a chocolate
cake comfortably.

As a young mother, I felt it my duty to go to
P.T.A. meetings. I remember standing in the Jane
Addams school foyer watching the other parents
easily talking to one another while I stood apart,
feeling alone.

I was probably forty-one or forty-two before I
turned the corner, saw life differently and began to

develop a positive attitude toward myself and the world. And I'm grateful to the people of Bainbridge Island for the opportunities they have provided to increase the feeling of well-being that is now an important part of my daily life.

I suspect what I have said sounds familiar in varying degrees to many, particularly women, of my generation. How does such a transition as I have described take place? Maybe the story of my life will furnish some clues.

When I think of my birth on a hot July day in 1908, I recall the story my parents told about Dad who ran coatless and tieless in Seattle down First Avenue from the hotel to the hospital to welcome me into the world.

I was named after both grandmothers, who had died before I was born. Phoebe Orlena Day/Spafford, my maternal grandmother, died of Bright's Disease six months before I arrived. Martha Cook had succumbed to consumption (tuberculosis) while Dad was a teenager. The disease also took his father, sister and later his brother, Kittredge.

My father, Charles Milton Cook, came from a German family originally named Von Koch. The name was changed when the family moved to England. Dad claims to have John Milton, the poet, as an ancestor, but I have never checked this out.

Dad was about five feet eleven, slender and fine-boned. When I knew him, the distinguishing feature of his head was a bald pate surrounded by fine curly hair. Mother described him as a "gentleman of the old school." A gentle man he certainly was, with quiet dignity relieved by a sense of humor. He liked to play practical jokes. Once during a hot summer in St. Paul, he tied limburger cheese to the bedsprings of some friends who were on vacation. By the time the Leonards came home, the cheese had already done its work. They took every item out of every drawer. They scrubbed the floor thoroughly. They stripped the closet and examined every piece of clothing. When they reported they were going to buy a new mattress because it was the only possible source of the odor, Dad confessed.

He was thirty-five when he married Mother who was his secretary and fifteen years younger. Until the babies came, she accompanied him when he travelled around the country as a bank and vault engineer, designing and supervising the building of bank interiors. Since he had left school at age thirteen to support his family, he was a self-educated man. At that time, it was not always necessary to have a degree in architecture or engineering to do a job.

When my sisters and I were little, Dad wasn't home very much, but when he was, he entertained us each evening with his guitar. He played by ear any tune that entered his head, even melodies from operas. When he played a particular march of his own composition, we three took off all our clothes and marched around the house until we or Dad became exhausted. Then up the stairs we climbed to pajamas and bed. Once, while we were marching around, I stumbled and sat down on the hot floor register. The square little burns needed a doctor. The embarrassment was almost too much.

Mother was third from the last of thirteen children, five of whom died at birth. I know about her position in the family because the way Grandmother called her children in from play, according to Mother, always amused me. It was as one word—Gertie-Annie-Edie-Artie-Helen. Mother was Edie. She was lovely to look at—long dark hair piled high, golden brown eyes, dusky skin and a well-proportioned figure. With her peers, she was full of fun. With us, well, we were a serious responsibility, She read a great deal, though because she had left school as a sophomore, she felt herself to be uneducated.

She had no outside activities. Like many homemakers of her day, she washed on Monday, ironed on Tuesday, cleaned on Wednesday, shopped on Thursday and baked on Saturday—pies, cookies and always beans. She didn't go to church, although she claimed to be a Baptist. But each Sunday she carefully dressed her girls and sent them off to Sunday school.

There was something about Mother that bothered me, although not my sisters. She was always right, it seemed. She had very clear standards of behaviour and expected everyone else to have them too, especially her chidren. We were overwhelmed by her values. At least I was. As I look back now, I see that many of them *were* right, and I am grateful, but some of them like racial prejudice and antagonism toward men (not Dad) I never felt good about, and later had to do some serious rethinking.

Since Dad was gone so much, Mother practically raised us. She was thorough, I will say. We were carefully dressed, especially at Easter when complete new outfits were the order of the day. They always included patent leather slippers, straw hats, gloves and lightweight coats. We wore navy pleated skirts with white square-collared middy blouses to school. I was the bane of my sisters' existence because I could keep one blouse clean for a whole week, while they had to change every day or two.

Spring was time for a large dose of sulphur and molasses. It was supposed to cleanse your system.

Mother fed us well, though peanut butter sandwiches and bananas for lunch everyday got a bit tiresome.

Our education went beyond public schools. We took swimming lessons, and when I was twelve, we finally settled down in one place long enough to buy a second-hand, carved upright piano with a revolving stool so we could take piano lessons. Harriet Stegner was our fat, jolly teacher, and before long, I was playing "Sparklets" and "Rustic Festival." We could take lessons as long as we practiced. My sisters soon got bored, but I loved it, and by the time I was fourteen was practicing four hours a day after school. Mother's father died that year, and I felt sorry for her as she mourned up in her room. What could I do? She might like to hear some piano, so I looked through my music and found Chopin's Funeral March. I started to play as expressively as I knew how, and she called down from upstairs, "Phoebe, quit that!" Well, I tried.

I always liked school, as far as subjects were concerned. I wasn't aggressive enough to be a top student, but I got mostly B grades. Arithmetic scared me, but I loved reading. I started early a lifelong habit of reading one book after another at home. I loved that arty Palmer Method of handwriting. I detested gym and those awful bloomers and gym suits and later, taking showers with other girls. I did pretty well writing stories. Oh, and I excelled in spelling.

I had an English teacher who wore a fluffy black wig. The students made fun of her, but not her teaching. She said she read every one of Dickens' books every year. Her specialty was Chaucer, and we actually learned to enjoy reading it.

Winters in Chicago we walked to school on top

of snow packed twenty feet high. In St. Paul, we sometimes skated to school on ice-covered sidewalks. We always lived in cities near school, so transportation was no problem. I think, though I'm not sure, that I went to kindergarten at the old Denny School in Seattle before the regrade because I remember a shortcut through the bushes and up a hill to a wooden staircase that climbed way up to the school at the top.

My sisters were one and a half and two and a half years younger than I. Jeanne, better known as Johnny because she was meant to be a son, could do and did strange twists with her body that always got a laugh. She could climb a tree higher than any boy. Once she threw a book at a teacher who made her sit in the back of the room. Later we learned she needed glasses. She would throw herself on the trolley track so the conductor would give her a quarter to get off. Her unladylike behaviour embarrassed me to tears often. In spite of that, I was her best audience. She always took care of me, and I loved her dearly.

Duckie was quite different. Do we always think baby sisters are spoiled? I thought she was. It seemed she could do no wrong, as far as Mother was concerned. She was very quick and had an answer for anything, usually a funny one. She could tell stories. I remember one she told on the screened sleeping porch where we all slept, about a mouse that ran around a corral on the back of an elephant. When she was born, she had thick curly hair, and the English nurse we had at the time called her, "the dear little duckie." That's where she got her nickname.

As you see, both sisters were attention getters. My system was to be a good little girl and play the piano. I once wrote a poem about that:

LITTLE LADY

Aroma of roast turkey
permeates the air
of our living room.

Aunt Mary and Uncle Charlie,
sleepy and replete, relax
in matching dusty rose wing-chairs.
Squeals of my sisters at play
out in the summer sun
arouse feelings of envy.

The old Weber piano sits
upright against
a wainscoated wall.
My unwilling hand
rotates the circle
of the piano stool.
"Humoresque" and "Sparklets"
fall from my reluctant fingers
on cool white keys.

I curtsy
and amuse my parents' guests
on command.
I am a little lady.

I wasn't always ladylike. Sometimes I broke
loose and did things I shouldn't. Occasionally, we
hung on to our Sunday school nickels and bought
jawbreakers with them, which, of course, had to be
eaten before we got home. Then once, when we were
teenagers, we had company for dinner. Probably in
order to enjoy their adult converstion, our parents
gave us money to go downtown and see a movie. Instead, we went to a burlesque show on First

160

Avenue, not realizing in advance how embarrassed we would be when the almost nude girls came dancing out the runway. We were surprised to see how few women and girls were in the audience. Another time, I hit Jeanne on the head with a shoetree not suspecting it had so much bounce it would cut her head open making it bleed. I'm afraid I was more concerned about her telling Mother than I was about her wound. She didn't tell.

Among the highlights of my early years were the trips I took with my dad on a steamboat that sailed between Seattle and San Francisco. Mother got sick even thinking about boats. Besides, she had two babies at home. So I had Dad all to myself. I remember running along the wooden decks with Dad behind trying to catch up.

When I was eight, it was a near tragedy when I almost lost two fingers on my right hand. We were playing house in the vestibule of the apartment house where we lived. I rested my hand on the door jamb and one of the kids closed the heavy entrance door. My fore and middle fingers hung by a strip of skin as the bones were broken. Fortunately, a nurse next door knew what to do and helped Mother get me to a doctor who managed to save the fingers. I think my life might have been quite different if I had not been able to play the piano.

At fourteen, before antibiotics almost eliminated such a thing, I had a mastoid. I had to go to the hospital and had what they called "brain fever." Coming out of the anesthetic following the ear-bone scraping, I thought I saw military tanks made out of weiners coming at me from the joint of ceiling and wall. When I finally went home, the neighbor kids had made a canopy of boughs for me to walk through from the car to the house. It certainly made me feel special. Because of the fever I had, my hair all fell out, and I wore a wide headband for a while. Again I felt special, in a less welcome way.

Mother wouldn't let me go out on a date until I was sixteen. I could go to mixed parties where we played spin-the-bottle and post office, but I couldn't go out alone with a boy. I had a special boyfriend, Neil McGinnis, who was as impatient for that July twelfth birthday to arrive as I was. When it did, Neil took me to a Barnum and Baily Circus. I wore a straight, pale blue, sleeveless dress, a white felt hat with a big brim, white pumps and white gloves. We took the bus to the circus where we twice rode the ferris wheel—our hearts in our mouths—ate pink cotton candy, shot the ducks and won a teddy bear. Neil kissed me on the cheek in the tunnel of love, and we felt very grown up.

My last high school year was at Broadway in Seattle. I got involved in music activities. The senior class produced *H.M.S. Pinafore* which I accompanied. I worked closely all year with my favorite teacher, Bryfie, who became my friend.

Graduation was at Meany Hall. I wore a lavendar georgette dress with a long waist and petals for a skirt. As accompanist for Harold to sing "Invictus" and for a girls' sextet to sing "Lift Thine Eyes," I was to sit on the stage. We stood at the bottom of the stairs, waiting for our entrance, holding our hands high so they would be nice and white for our public.

The following summer was terrible. I didn't know what to do. Jobs for no-skills, scared girls were not to be found. I applied for one job as an accompanist. I reached a downtown office, and when I walked in, a man closed the door, and told me to

162

take off my hat. Naive as I was, it didn't take me long to realize he had more on his mind than music, and I got out of there in a hurry.

Finally, in September Mother said, "How would you like to go to college?" I wanted to, but hadn't asked because it hadn't occurred to me it was possible. "We'll go see what Dad says," said Mother. He was in bed with what he called "quinsy," a sore throat. He was sitting up and had a medicated towel around his neck. When Mother asked her question, Dad said, "Why would a *girl* want to go to college?" "Don't you think Phoebe might make a good teacher?" she answered. He agreed we could try it for a year and see what happened. Mother and I went out to the University of Washington to get me registered, and I was given ten credits for my piano training. The day school started, I met some Broadway classmates at the bus stop on Broadway and Pine. They didn't know I would be there, so it was quite a reunion.

I liked the studies in college, especially music, but socially, I was a dud. I had one girlfriend, Dee Tinkcom. We were together constantly. I had one boyfriend named Bill, a sweet, quiet fellow. Both were sort of private friends, not part of a group. That lasted until my junior year. Then one night, Dee broke a date with me, and I realized I had few if any other resources, and I'd had it being lonely.

So one day, I gathered up my courage and went to see the Dean of Women, May Dunn Ward. I told her my problem, and she immediately set me down to write invitations to about a dozen independent women to meet and discuss organizing a social group for girls who were not sorority members. She had been thinking about this for a long time, and the people she had selected were all, except me, outstanding on campus in one way or another. We started Phrateres which still exists at the University of Washington. I have lost touch and have no idea what it is like now, but at the time, it enriched the lives of many young women who wanted to learn something of campus life outside of books and classes. I made lifelong friends, developed social skills, and fun became a part of college life.

I was lucky to be able to finish college in June, 1930, because in October, 1929, the stock market crashed, and the world fell apart. Dad lost his job, along with millions of others. He was almost sixty, so he never worked again, except to do odd jobs like repairing safes.

Because of the Depression, I was lucky, too, to get a teaching job. Many of my classmates did not. The first year I taught, I earned $140 a month. My fourth and last year, my salary was $68. I was hired to teach both high school and grade school music, freshman English, public speaking, business law and to coach girls' basketball. The school was a consolidated one of five hundred students of all grades in Winlock, Washington, the "egg capital of the world." Sometimes the town was called Finnlock because of the large number of its Finnish people.

I was quite unprepared for life away from a structured home. I had to learn to make decisions for myself, not always wise ones. For instance, I was more comfortable with the high school students than with the much older teaching staff, so I fraternized a bit. I directed and accompanied a senior male quartet of boys nearly my age. We performed at schools, neighboring towns, Grange meetings, church affairs and parties. Also, I had a warm hearted student friend, Leona Brewer, who was my liaison with the community. To my surprise, at the end of my first year, I was released by the superintendent who himself was fired for embezzling funds from the Ford Company in town. The new superintendent came to see me in Seattle during the summer and hired me back.

I lived in a boarding house near school with mostly women teachers, and shared a room with Lila McConnaghy who later married the science teacher, Detlef Jans. The fourth year I went down to breakfast on the first day of school, and there sat two new men. Jerry planned to be in town a short time doing some sort of survey. Actually he drove onto a bridge over a river when it was flooding and was drowned. The other man, Al Smith, tall, colorful and single, had been transferred by the Union Oil Company from Kelso to Winlock as a tank truck salesman.

One night a group of us went over to the Olequa River to build a fire on the bank and roast weiners and marshmallows. Al and I left the group for a stroll along the river, sat down in the moonlight, and he told me of his dream to cruise around the world in a sailboat. He stopped for a moment and asked, "Do you want to go with me?" "Sure," I said, taking him seriously. That night I wrote Mother to tell her I thought I had met the man I was going to marry and that he had the most beautiful voice she would ever hear. A month later we were engaged, and in March, we eloped to Shelton and were married by a justice of the peace—a pretty short romance, considering the fifty-three years so far that we have been married.

We eloped for two reasons: one, my teaching contract forbade me to marry because I was a woman, and two, I was afraid Mother would not approve and would try to talk me out of it. She still had visions of me as a professional woman. On a sunny Saturday in 1934, a St. Patrick's Day, we drove from Shelton, after the ceremony, to Mt. Rainier to meet with friends the next day for skiing, the only time I have ever skied. We didn't tell anyone we were married until after school was out and we moved to Centralia.

I think I had read too many fairy tales that ended, "They got married and lived happily ever after." At first I thought "living happily" would take care of itself, but it didn't work out that way. I had a lot to learn. We both did. To that point, I had used my hands for playing piano. Now I had to use them for cooking, cleaning and making out budgets. Al knew little about money. He'd always had it. Now we didn't. Those years were a struggle. But they were fun too and an adventure. And instead of being an ending, they were a beginning to an entirely new kind of life.

In two years, Sylvia Chesley was born, delivered by Dr. Toothacher. Jeanne drove down from Seattle in a blizzard with the cedar chest she had made, painted white and decorated with a huge black face of Mickey Mouse on top. As she often did, she operated on intuition and drove down on an impulse, arriving at the same time Sylvia did.

Shortly after Sylvia was born, Al lost his job and could find only pickup work like shovelling streets when there was snow.

We rented a little five room house at 107 Cherry Street for $15 a month. It had wood burning stoves in the kitchen and dining rooms. For furniture, we had a bed that dipped toward the middle in one bedroom and a crib in the other. My piano, the Weber I'd had since I was sixteen, and a rocker furnished the living room, and a small dropleaf table rotated between kitchen and dining room. That was it.

Food was hard to come by. I remember lots of split pea soup. Once we were appalled when potatoes, stored in a cooler, froze. Often we charged baby food and fruit for Sylvia with the kindly, bald-headed, corner grocer and paid him when we could. For ourselves, we made do with what we had.

Finally, when Sylvia was a year and a half, we decided to move to Seattle where we could share our problems with my parents. We sold everything except my piano—even Al's banjo, for which he got six dollars. We drove to Seattle, glad to leave Centralia behind, and found a housekeeping room with twin beds and a two-burner plate. Sylvia slept in a dresser drawer.

From a rough beginning, matters gradually improved until in three or four years, we were able to buy a comfortable house in the Ravenna district. It cost $3,500, and we made the down payment of $500 by borrowing money from a Canadian bank with the help of a note signed by a friend.

I didn't have a washing machine until we'd been married six years. I washed clothes, including diapers, in the bathtub and usually hung them outside to dry. I can still see my first washer—round and green, with curved legs and a wringer rotated by hand. I don't remember being unhappy because we were poor. Of course, many other people were even worse off than we were. We just took it all in stride. Anyway, I've always liked a challenge, and we certainly had that.

Besides, I had three little girls to keep me busy—Sylvia born in 1936; Susan, in 1939; Jennifer, 1946. This was another challenge, an absorbing one. We did the best we knew how, though there were times when we wondered if we really knew what we were doing. What do you do when your child, dressed in a chenille robe, backs into a fireplace fire? or falls down the basement stairwell and cracks her head open trying to imitate the big kids? or gets into a jeep with a group of men who offer to drive her to school, feeling perfectly safe because "they were soldiers"? or moves her bed next door because it was "time she became independent"? or drives the Model A ford into the ditch across the street while she was backing out of the garage to take a little practice ride before her mother got home? You just take one step at a time and hope you've done the right thing.

When Susan was three, she seemed far too dependent on me. I started a nursery school in the church on the corner so she could learn from other children her own age. This was during World War II, so not only did Susan benefit, but I was doing my share for the war effort. And I learned more about children, among other things, preparing them for change. We had a new playhouse delivered one day and set it up in the corner of the room. The immediate reaction of the little boys was to urinate in the flower boxes. After that, we warned them when something new was going to take place.

Mother said she thought the girls should have a Sunday school education. I looked all around the neighborhood to find a small intimate church environment for them and settled on the Unitarian Church School. We liked the idea of their learning about different religions without being indoctrinated, hoping that later they would work out belief systems for themselves, which they did. I worked with them in the Sunday school and eventually became its director.

Al was out of town often, so I was alone with

the children. I had too much time and curiosity to stay home all the time, even though "Woman's place is in the home" was the credo for the day. He didn't question my decisions usually, though when the girls were about seven and ten, he complained that he wasn't getting enough attention. Actually, he left home. I was devastated and wandered around the house half aware and sometimes unable to breathe. A week later, he came to the back door, threw his hat on the floor thinking if I didn't throw out the hat, I probably wouldn't throw him out either. "May I come in and talk about starting over?" he said. I needed that break in our relationship to learn to keep a better balance in our lives.

I continued, on a more controlled scale, to involve myself in activities that could be shared with the girls. I taught group piano lessons and studied at Cornish to learn how. Sylvia and I worked on a children's radio program, "Little Miss Muffet." She learned a song and was interviewed by Mother Goose (Ola Todd) each week. I provided music for the show. It was wartime, and our scripts were carefully inspected before each performance. I didn't see how we could have upset the war effort even if we had wanted to, but that's the way it was. When Sylvia started to kindergarten and the other children teased her about Little Miss Muffet, she wanted to stop doing the program, so we did.

Again I became over-involved. I was trying to keep a husband happy, make a home, direct a nursery school and a church school, all at the same time. One day I felt a tight band around my waist, and my feet felt like pins and needles that seemed to raise me off the ground. The problem didn't go away, so I went to Dr. Eddy who was also a friend. The cause, apparently, was not physical but emotional. After some months of counseling, I learned I didn't *have* to do everything anyone expected of me, and I could relax inside even when I was busy. Though there have been times since then when I tended to overdo, I have managed to avoid extremes that lead to trouble.

As the girls got older, I had more time. When they were nineteen, sixteen and nine, I returned to teaching. After a couple of years substituting at Jane Addams Junior High in Seattle, I found myself teaching almost every day, most often for men math teachers, and Al asked, "Why don't you get a teaching job of your own? It might be easier." I followed his suggestion and looked around. I could have taught handicapped children at a junior high, eighth grade English at a Jewish school or grade three at View Ridge Elementary School. I chose the last because it presented the least stress, and I still had a family at home.

I thoroughly enjoyed my sixteen years at View Ridge. I was finally doing something that used all the skills I had developed and more. Three sixth grade teachers were men who preferred not to teach their own music, so I moved to sixth grade and we did exchanges—music for math, science and spelling. I had a glee club of a hundred sixth graders who gave concerts at Christmas and in the spring. The last few years, I had the privilege of being a demonstration teacher. About twelve or fifteen selected teachers from throughout the city visited our classroom where the students and I showed how we operated in Room 17. Once we had been studying Europe and North Africa. Each child had been assigned a different country and would research one subject at a time: food, dress, religion, education, etc. and report to the class. The day of the demonstration, they reported their findings on dress. Some wore the costume of the countries. Some brought dolls. Others brought pictures, either real or verbal.

One of the parents was having trouble communicating with her daughter about sex. She asked if anything could be done in class to answer her girl's questions. *She* certainly couldn't. I told my principal and asked if it would be appropriate to get the parents together to discuss the matter. He said no other teacher had asked to do this, but if I wanted to, I should go ahead. The mother and I invited the other parents to a meeting in her home. Most came, even fathers. We roughly designed a unit of study which later I refined. I don't remember now what it contained, but after the study, parents thanked me, and more than one student said, "I just haven't been able to discuss this with Mom." I thought then, and I think now that close parent-teacher cooperation is invaluable to a good education.

Meanwhile in the family, Sylvia socialized her way through high school, then was selected a princess for the annual Lake City Pioneer Days celebration. She wrapped herself in her role as sister to a reigning monarch and took part in community affairs and finally the parade. She had her first experience with the news media when she was interviewed by a reporter. The resulting article had little resemblance to what she had actually said, much to the surprise of all of us.

Susan came home from school one day and asked, "Mom, shall I be a rink (street-wise person) or a student?" She had decided she couldn't or wouldn't compete with Sylvia's life style. She chose to be a scholar and became a good one all the way through a master's degree in economics and beyond. She demonstrated this choice when she was the only student in her high school American history class to respond to the teacher's invitation to join a neighborhood precinct meeting to see first hand how government works, and worked through a campaign.

In the eighth grade, Jennifer was one of a girls' quartet, the Chantones, that won a cup at a Ballard community festival. Later, on her seventeenth birthday, we split the cost of a $100 guitar with her. She was fascinated with the coffee houses in the University district, popular in the sixties, where she played her guitar and met and later married a Canadian folk singer.

Throughout those years when all of us busied ourselves living our lives separately and jointly, Al tried his best to give us the support of all kinds that we needed. Because he and I had grown up in an age of innocence, we found raising teenagers in the fifties and sixties to be confusing and sometimes difficult. However, we must have done something right because they all matured into fine productive women.

When they were all on their own but Jennifer, we finally bought the sailboat Al had dreamed of all his life. It was a thirty-eight foot Monk-designed ketch with a wooden hull and a twenty-five-horsepower gasoline engine that got us into trouble later. We sailed whenever we could and spent a great deal of time preparing the boat and ourselves for the trip we planned down the west coast, through the Panama Canal and into the Caribbean. We needed ceiling hand-holds, a gimballed stove, dodgers for the stern and many other items to make life safer and more comfortable for the journey.

We reached a point when we couldn't wait any

longer. We were ready to set sail. I took a sabbatical leave from teaching. Al quit his job. We rented the house. The students and teachers had farewell parties. Then with some friends, Glen and Marian Fairbanks, we took off on June 6, 1965. The events of that trip are another story that nearly ended in tragedy. The boat blew up in Acapulco. We sold what was left of it to an Uruguayan who gave us a bad check. We continued on our journey by bus. The Tica bus line from Guatalama City took us to the capital of each Central American country, where we stayed a while. Eventually, we reached Panama, and after exploring it a bit, we flew home. It took us eleven months to reach Panama and eleven hours to get back home.

We resumed our work lives for a few years during which we built a cruiser we could live on. I told Al I'd try to live on the boat if I could have a new piano aboard. We bought a Yamaha studio-size piano and bolted it to an inside wall and to the cabin sole. Al put a forty-watt light bulb inside the piano, and when we moved it to a house eight years later, it barely needed tuning. That piano is still my pride and joy.

During the time we lived aboard at F dock at Shilshole Bay Marina in Seattle, Al retired and offered to cook the meals, as I was still working. For two years, I came home after school and flopped on the davenport while he got dinner. He was a gourmet cook which was expensive but pleasant.

We were still living on the boat when I retired in 1971. I thought when I left teaching, I would miss it because I enjoyed it so much. I hardly took a backware glance. There were just so much to do, and places to go.

Of all the travelling we did in the next ten

years—Mexico repeatedly; to Alaska on our boat; to England; to Hawaii twice; to Yugoslavia and Italy by freighter—certainly the most unique was a leisurely drive down the length of the Baja Peninsula before there was a road. We travelled in a green G.M. truck with ten inch tires. Al had built three bunks (Granddaughter Heidi, 14, came along) with storage underneath. We set table on the tailgate and cooked on two primus stoves borrowed from the boat; they needed the least fuel. A shower bag hung outside the truck. All we had to do was turn a little valve, and we got a welcome trickle of water. A useful piece of equipment was a plywood cube of two and a half feet that made a seat, a small table, or, with the lid lifted, a toilet. The spare tire was stored on top the cab, and that's where Heidi often sat to give us directions.

We had learned from the small amount of written material on Baja available in 1971 that there was a strip of highway, such as it was, on the northwest coast of Baja and again on the southeast coast. We could expect nothing in between except some sandy or rocky trails. We could travel about eight or ten miles an hour—maybe. We learned that it would be hot and dry and that the town you saw on a map might be no more than a house or two. Places to get water or gasoline or even food were rare, so we would need to carry a supply of all three. And it would be a good idea to have a felt hat to strain gas in when it *was* available.

At night, the stars were brighter and closer than we had ever seen them. The desert without people was quiet, and we would have been lonesome except that we had each other. In spite of this, Heidi got out of bed one night to reclaim her cosmetic case from the tailgate because she "didn't want any hoodlums to steal it."

Toward the end of the trip, we camped on a sandbar, La Requeson, and sat under a large beach umbrella watching Heidi splash in the water. Al was concerned that she would get sunburned but forgot he himself was at risk. His feet were in the shade, but the reflection of the sun on white sand burned them anyway. They swelled to twice their normal size, so we had to get to La Paz. He could barely drive, but he had to as I wasn't driving at the time. We reached the town not only sunburned but hot, thirsty, dirty and miserable. Fortunately, the manager of a luxury hotel, Los Arcos, took one pitying look at us, and for $14 a night, rented us a cool room with an alcove for Heidi and a large tiled shower. That night we sipped margueritas and dined in style on an open, flower-trimmed patio, attended by white clad waiters and serenaded by a Mariachi trio.

In 1975, we moved to Bainbridge to guard the outstation of Seattle's Queen City Yacht Club of which we were members. We fell in love with the island and its friendly people and decided this was where we wanted to live the rest of our lives. Boat living changed to mobile home living. Plans to build a log cabin in the woods never materialized.

Through a friend, I was invited to help with the Bainbridge Light Opera group, now called Bainbridge Performing Arts (B.P.A.), whose summer musical was to be "Down In the Valley." Although I was nervous at first, I stayed with the summer shows for twelve years. Each winter we went south to California or Mexico for a few months, but hurried back in the spring so I could work on the show. The most demanding musical was *Music Man* because I was the only pianist. The most fun was

Oklahoma which featured two pianos and a small orchestra. I still play for B.P.A. auditions and shows once in a while.

One day I wandered into Helpline to see what it was all about and found there a cousin, Connie Kemp, and a cordial group of warm-hearted people. I got involved as a regular volunteer, and for six years, worked on employment, matching people who needed work with others who needed help.

When I was no longer president of the Senior Center, I told Al I would like to do something I could handle at home. He said, "Why don't you try your hand at writing; You've always enjoyed that." Little did he know at the time that he would become my continuing listener and critic. By some miracle of timing, the next day I got a phone call from Theresa Morrow, then news editor of the *Bainbridge Review,* asking me to write a weekly column, "Senior Newsmakers", containing stories and pictures about interesting oldsters on the island.

I enjoyed doing this until Al developed a gangrenous foot and some internal problems, and I dropped all my activities except a writing lab, to become a nurse. He expected to lose a leg, maybe both, and because of that and medication, was deeply depressed. I never expected to hear him say he didn't want to live but that's the way he felt at the time. I don't know when I've been so confused. Walking pneumonia took hold, and it was all I could do to go between home and the hospital each day. However, the doctors were able to save his leg, and he began to heal both physically and mentally. The year following was one of the best of our lives together because just being alive and whole had taken on a new value.

About the time I began the column for the

newspaper, I had started with a small group of dedicated writers, several of whom have already published, in a workshop led by Nancy Rekow. It and she are a source of not only inspiration but motivation. The need to write something for the group to read almost every week really keeps the ink flowing. This has been going on for several years now, and I hope it continues for a long time.

I've tried several types of writing—short stories, a novel never finished, children's stories, articles—but I feel best writing about real people. Thus, the series of autobiographical oral histories of which this story is one.

I'm still involved in Bainbridge Senior Center and do public relations for the Board. We both feel at home at the Center and have made some fine friends.

We enjoy them and other friends, every-day life and our family. Sylvia is no longer a butterfly but a serious artist. Susan is trying to adjust to the loss of a son killed in an automobile accident. Jennifer became a Canadian and an artist.

One regret sometimes surfaces—that I have not often enough given the time and effort to address directly the serious ongoing problems of the world I live in—hunger, poverty, homelessness, child abuse, mental and other illnesses. I could have been more involved in these issues. In fairness to myself, I admit to reasons for not having given these matters priority. Nevertheless, I have regrets, because if people like me don't do it, who will? Maybe in the next world or another life. Who knows?

I celebrated my seventy-ninth birthday last summer and fell into a brief depression when I realized I would soon be eighty. I've always thought of people in their eighties as being old—set apart. I do not think of myself as old—certainly not set apart. True, I get tired a little sooner than I used to. I've slowed down a bit. I'd rather stay home at night now. I don't eat quite as much. I say "no" more often. If that means I've reached the top rungs of the ladder, so be it. Most of the time it feels good to be there and to look back and around and say, "I'm fortunate. Life is full of satisfaction with my family, my world and myself."

What They Say

Alice Tawresey—Mayor of Winslow:
"Amazing richness of detail, emotion and mood create a longing to return to a simpler time."

Theresa Morrow—journalist:
"Seining with horses, seances in Italy, shooting prairie dogs in New Mexico prove once and for all that history need not be a dreary thing."

Carl Berg—banker:
"A splendid idea, compressing over 800 years of living onto a few pages—what a reference for young people to learn how life was lived before their time."

Anne Fleming—actress:
"Delightful reading. These memoirs transport one back to a less frantic era filled with drama, courage and humor—all the ingredients of a good play."

Bainbridge
Island
Senior
Community
Center

. . . open a new door . . .

ISBN 0-9620506-1-X